MAKING
MINIATURES

MAKING MINIATURES

IN ¹⁄₁₂ SCALE

VENUS &
MARTIN DODGE

A **DAVID & CHARLES** CRAFT BOOK

British Library Cataloguing in Publication Data
Dodge, Venus
    Making miniatures: in 1/12 scale.–
    (A David & Charles craft book)
    1. Miniatures objects. Making
    I. Title   II. Dodge, Martin
    745.592

    ISBN 0-7153-9106-2 H/B
    ISBN 0-7153-9963-2 P/B

    First published 1989
    Reprinted 1990 (three times)
    Reprinted 1991

    First published in paperback 1991

    Reprinted 1993, 1994

Typeset by ABM Typographics Ltd., Hull
and printed in Singapore by
C. S. Graphics Pte Ltd.

for David & Charles
Brunel House   Newton Abbot   Devon

Distributed in the United States by
Sterling Publishing Co. Inc.
387 Park Avenue South, New York, NY 10016-8810

CONTENTS

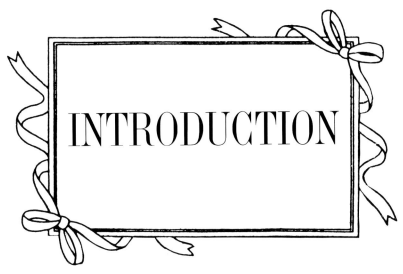

INTRODUCTION

Once upon a time, anyone over the age of twelve who was interested in dolls' houses and miniatures was regarded as mildly eccentric, but in recent years there has been a rapid growth of interest in miniatures, and miniaturists come in all shapes and sizes and both sexes. Once it was almost impossible to find even a sheet of wallpaper in the right scale, but now there are shops and suppliers everywhere catering to the needs of both the DIY enthusiast and the collector. It is not surprising that making or collecting miniatures has become such a popular hobby because it offers an outlet for a wide range of interests and abilities – from the child who models in self-hardening clay to the skilled needlewoman or the craftsman who works in wood: there is something for everyone.

The scope of interest is widening all the time, moving away from the dolls' house and into room sets, vignettes, models and even fantasies. Though dolls' houses are still immensely popular, there is now much more to miniatures than houses. The dolls' house, while it offers a splendid place to display miniatures, can limit the range of things one makes or collects for it – through lack of space or because many items would be out of place in a house. The current trend is towards miniature 'projects' – perhaps a room set or a model, complete in itself, where the imagination can be given free rein, without the restrictions imposed by a dolls' house. Three room sets might be wildly different in style and period – unsatisfactory in a house which is viewed as a whole but perfectly acceptable as three separate rooms; and a mermaid which would look most odd in a house, can look perfectly at home in a goldfish bowl!

This book offers a variety of projects for a range of abilities, beginning with simple shoebox rooms designed for children and working up to large room settings complete with fine furniture. Many of the projects may be made for a dolls' house and we hope that miniaturists whose main interest is domestic will find plenty of useful ideas. Anyone who does not have a dolls' house nor wishes to make one will find plenty of alternatives such as a shop, a potting shed or a garden.

We have included some more unusual items like the deckchair, ladder and tailor's dummy, as well as conventional furniture and we hope that we have found something to please everyone. We have also used a few kits, which are now widely available, and a variety of miniature accessories from specialist suppliers and craftsmen. We believe that most miniaturists are interested in both making and collecting, and we hope that this book, although it is mainly a guide to making miniatures, will also demonstrate the wide range of fine ready-made pieces that are now available. Full details of these items are given and there is a comprehensive list of suppliers at the back of the book. We have also listed the dates and venues of the larger miniatures fairs around the UK. We hope that these lists of suppliers and fairs will be of particular interest to our overseas readers who may be planning visits to Britain. British miniatures have gained a worldwide reputation for quality and most miniaturists like to include a fair and some shopping in their visit to this country.

The book concentrates, however, on making miniatures, and we have used the ¹/₁₂ (1in to 1ft) scale throughout as this is now the accepted standard scale. The smaller ¹/₁₆ scale is still used for commercial dolls' houses and miniatures designed for children, but is rarely found in collectors' miniatures.

Anyone who has made pieces from our earlier *The Dolls' House DIY Book* should have no difficulty with the earlier projects in this book, which have been designed to appeal to beginners, but we hope that as your skill and confidence develop, you will find projects to keep pace with you, and that experienced miniaturists will enjoy making the furniture in the 'Edwardian Bedroom' and 'Farmhouse Kitchen'.

In Chapter 1, you will find a full discussion of materials and tools, including power tools, and basic methods of construction. The following chapters offer a wide variety of projects which use the materials, tools and methods described in Chapter 1; the complexity of the projects increases as the book progresses. This is however a guide and not a book of rules. We offer the methods that we use, but don't be afraid to experiment and 'do your own thing'.

First and foremost, making miniatures should be fun, and everyone who creates something is making something unique. What you make will be your taste, your skill, your miniature!

1 WORKING WITH WOOD

MAKING ROOM BOXES

PLYWOOD · With the exception of the simple shoebox rooms described in Chapter 2 and the mermaids in Chapter 3, all the projects in this book are made of plywood. The Daler board we used for several projects in the *The Dolls' House DIY Book* is no longer available, and as this book concentrates on the larger $1/12$ scale, plywood, with its greater strength, it is the most suitable medium. As none of the projects require a great deal of wood, the expense is small and we recommend that you buy the best quality you can afford. The best plywood for room boxes is birch-faced ply. Until recently, this was available from most DIY shops, but it is becoming more difficult to find. If your local DIY shop cannot help, try a ship's chandler which will be able to supply marine ply, which is more expensive but will produce good results and save you time and effort in sanding and finishing. If you cannot find birch-faced ply, buy the best-looking piece of plywood you can find. Check through the shop's stock until you find a piece which is not warped (hold the piece in front of you at eye level and sight along the edges. If each edge is straight, then the board is flat.) The patterns for each project show the amount of plywood needed for its completion and you may find that your local shop sells plywood off-cuts in convenient sizes – large sheets can be awkward to transport and to handle.

BASIC TOOLS · To make a vignette or room box, you will need some basic woodworking tools. Firstly, a saw. The type we use and recommend is a rip-style saw, made for both rip sawing (cutting along the grain) and cross sawing (cutting across the grain of the wood). This will cut the plywood into the pieces you need to assemble a project, though the edges will be rough and will later need to be planed or sanded smooth. To cut plywood, draw the outline of the pieces to be cut onto the wood, using a sharp pencil and a metal ruler. Cut these pieces fractionally proud of the drawn line and plane or sand them smoothly to the line.

Although a plane is not absolutely essential, it does save a great deal of time and effort. A small block plane is easily handled in one hand, leaving the other hand free to support the wood.

To cut windows and doorways, use a 12in fret-saw with No 3 or 4 blades. The 12in throat is large enough to cut all the openings in the projects in this book. Draw the opening to be cut out onto the relevant piece, then drill a small hole in each corner – any type of drill may be used for this purpose – and insert the fret-saw blade through the hole (Fig 1). With a little practice, very straight lines can be sawn with a fret-saw, so aim to cut along the drawn line. The cut edges may then be sanded if necessary.

BASIC ASSEMBLY · The vignettes and room boxes are assembled with simple butt joints which are pinned, using 1in veneer pins, and white woodwork glue. Instructions for each project give full details of how each box is assembled (Fig 2 shows a typical assembly). The pieces are butt jointed, glued along the edges, and pins are tapped in at approximately 3in intervals. When the box is assembled, a thorough sanding with medium, then fine grade sandpaper both inside and out will prepare the surface for decoration.

DECORATING · Ordinary household emulsion paints, either silk or matt finish, may be applied directly to the wood, but on the inside are better applied over lining paper. The small sample pots of paint are a boon to the miniature decorator. Lining or wallpapers are applied with ordinary household wallpaper paste. Size the wall first with a watered coat of paste, allow it to dry, then paste the wallpaper and hang it. A large range of miniature wallpapers are now available from specialist suppliers or you might prefer to use wrapping-paper or small-patterned life-size wallpaper. Ceilings also have a smoother finish if they are lined before painting. The front edges of most projects are finished with a frame of wood-strip. This is $3/8$in wide wood, $1/8$in thick and is available in 3ft lengths from art and craft shops. The corners of each frame are mitred and a small mitre block (from DIY shops) makes the job a great deal easier.

WINDOWS · Windows in the projects in Chapters 8, 9, 10 and 11 are all made in basically the same way. They are constructed of spruce and $1/8$in perspex. Most art and craft shops and model shops stock a range of wood-strips in spruce and obeche – it is not expensive and it is a good

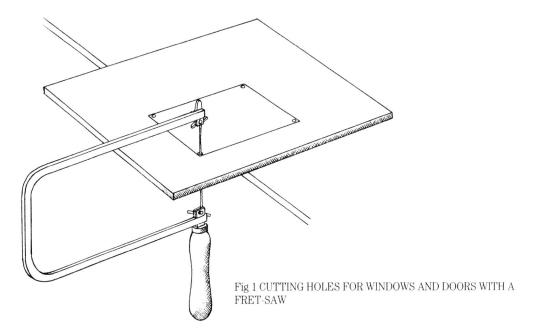

Fig 1 CUTTING HOLES FOR WINDOWS AND DOORS WITH A FRET-SAW

idea to buy a selection of sizes. The most useful sizes are ⅛in square, ⅛ x ½in, ⅛ x 3in and 3/32 x 3in. These are all available in 3ft lengths. Thin perspex, sold in model shops as Lexan sheet, is used for model cars and aeroplanes. For realism, this very thin perspex is desirable.

The windows are made by facing the edges of the window opening with ⅛in spruce (Fig 3a). Then a frame of ⅛in square wood-strip is glued into the window opening, at the outside edge (Fig 3b). The perspex is cut to size with a craft knife and fitted behind the frame with a little glue. A second frame of wood-strip is then fitted behind the perspex (Fig 3c). If the window is to be divided into two or three casements, the mullions, which are cut in ⅛in strips, are glued to the perspex as part of the frame. Then each casement is framed in 1/16in strip. Finally, vertical and horizontal glazing bars are stuck to

the perspex (Fig 3d). We find that double-sided Sellotape is a far neater way of fixing these tiny pieces than glue. Stick one side of the tape firmly to the wood-strip, then cut the pieces to size – through both wood and tape – peel off the tape backing and stick the piece to the perspex.

Patterns are given in each project for windows, but care should be taken to ensure that mullions and glazing bars are accurately spaced. It is easier to paint window frames in situ, but paint the glazing bars before they are stuck in place. The figures show how the windows are constructed – study them carefully before you begin. The windows in the projects in Chapters 10 and 11 both have window-sills, and instructions for these are given in the appropriate chapters.

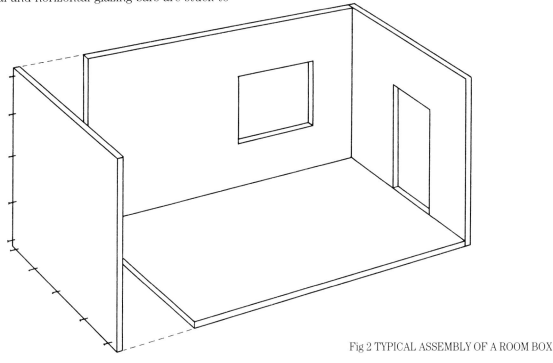

Fig 2 TYPICAL ASSEMBLY OF A ROOM BOX

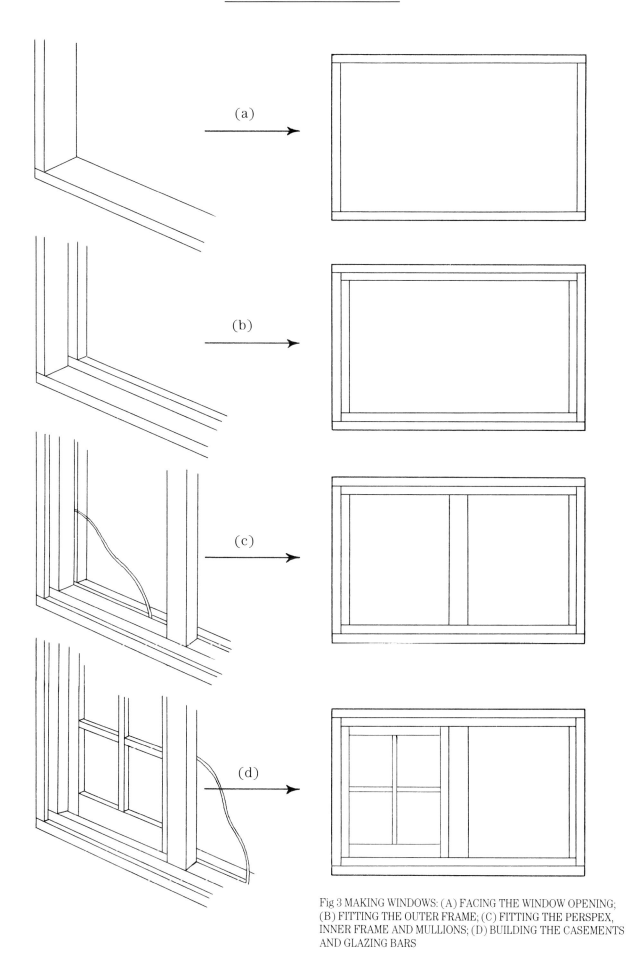

Fig 3 MAKING WINDOWS: (A) FACING THE WINDOW OPENING; (B) FITTING THE OUTER FRAME; (C) FITTING THE PERSPEX, INNER FRAME AND MULLIONS; (D) BUILDING THE CASEMENTS AND GLAZING BARS

DOORS · The method for making doors – whether they are made to open or not – is basically the same for all projects. The door hole is cut with a fret-saw and the edges are sanded smooth and faced with ⅛in wood-strip glued in place to the sides and top. A second frame of ⅛in square strip is then glued to this frame (see Fig 4). This second frame contains the door and permits it to open in only one direction. The doors are made from 3in wide spruce strip, 1/16in thick. Two basic types of door have been used: the panelled door and the planked and braced door.

To make a panelled door, cut a piece of 1/16in thick spruce to fit into the door case. The fit should not be tight, but should allow a fractional gap all the way around. Consider the floor covering and make allowance for sufficient clearance if the door is to open over it.

The panelling is built up on both sides of the door using

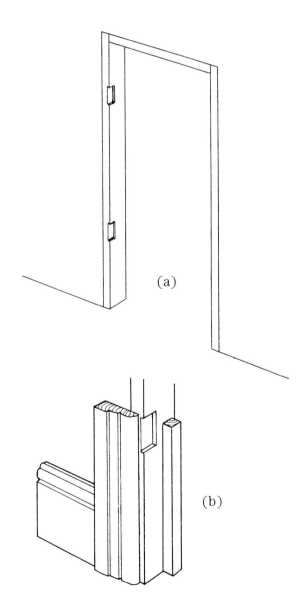

(a)

(b)

Fig 4 MAKING THE DOOR-FRAME: (A) FACING THE DOOR OPENING; (B) BUILDING UP THE INNER FRAME AND THE ARCHITRAVE AND SKIRTING-BOARD

1/16in spruce planed or sanded down to 1/32in thick. This will give an overall thickness to the door of ⅛in which is credibly realistic (see Fig 5a).

The planked door may be simply made by cutting a piece of 1/16in or 3/32in wood to fit the door case and scoring planks onto the wood with a craft knife, or, more realistically, by butt jointing separate planks. If the door is to be stained rather than painted, the latter method is recommended as it gives a more convincing result.

The braces are cut in 3/32in thick wood and glued onto the planked door (see Fig 5b).

The door used in the 'Farmhouse Kitchen' (see p157, Chapter 11) is more complicated and full instructions for making it are given in that chapter.

The doors are hinged with commercial miniature brass hinges 5/16in long (see list of stockists, pp175-9). To fit them, rest the hinge in place on the door and mark around it with a craft knife. Cut a shallow rebate to accommodate the hinge. The rebate should be of sufficient depth for half the barrel of the hinge to be accommodated. Glue the hinge into the rebate with either Superglue or epoxy resin. Fit the door in place and carefully mark the position of the hinge on the door case with a craft knife. Cut the rebate and glue the other half of the hinge in place. If you have never done this before, practise first with some scrap wood and spare hinges. The commercial hinges provide holes for pins, but pinning the hinges in place is very tricky and glueing them is perfectly satisfactory (see Fig 5c).

PAINTING · The doors and windows have been framed with commercial mouldings (see list of stockists), and the woodwork painted with Humbrol enamel paints. Sand thoroughly, then paint on one coat of matt white; this will raise the grain and, when it is dry, it should be thoroughly sanded again with 320-grit abrasive paper until it is perfectly smooth. Paint on a coat of either gloss or matt in your chosen colour and allow it to dry thoroughly. Sand again with 320-grit abrasive paper, remove all traces of dust and apply a final coat of paint. Good quality artists' brushes which do not shed hairs are essential for this job and use the paint as sparingly as possible so that it does not build up a thick coat, which might cause doors to stick.

Where an aged look is required on paintwork, follow the above directions to achieve a well-painted finish, then use fine sandpaper to gently rub down the paintwork to simulate wear in areas where such wear would naturally occur. This method works very well when used with matt finish paint (see the 'Farmhouse Kitchen', pp 154-5).

MAKING FURNITURE

The furniture projects range from very simple pieces, like those used in the shoebox rooms, to authentic Windsor chairs. The simpler pieces require only a modicum of skill and some basic tools, while the Windsor chairs should provide a challenge for skilled craftsmen.

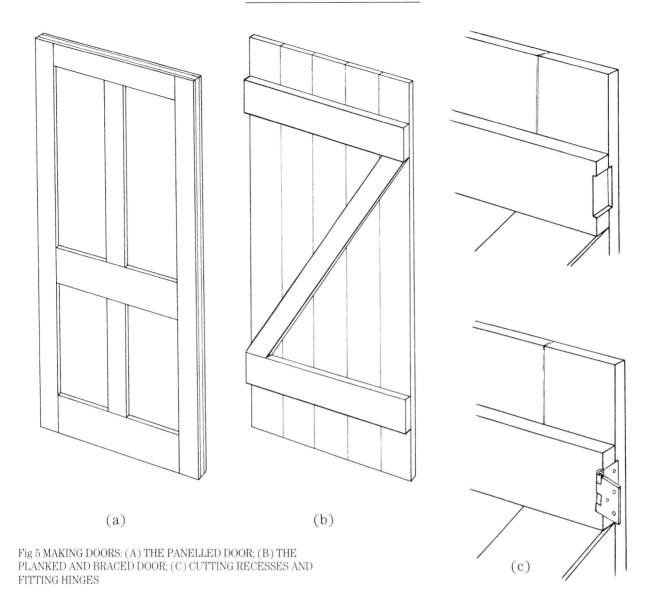

(a)   (b)   (c)

Fig 5 MAKING DOORS: (A) THE PANELLED DOOR; (B) THE
PLANKED AND BRACED DOOR; (C) CUTTING RECESSES AND
FITTING HINGES

BASIC TOOLS · The novice furniture-maker will require only the basic tools. First, a craft knife and a selection of blades, which are available from art and craft shops. We recommend two types – the Swan-Morton knife with No 1 blade and the X-acto knife with a selection of blades – we suggest No 11, fine-pointed blade, No 10, curved blade and No 17, chisel blade. These knives can be used for shaping, carving and, with a metal ruler, can be used to cut straight edges in a variety of materials.

A razor-toothed saw, from craft shops, is a small saw with a comfortable handle which will enable you to cut the wooden pieces needed to assemble the furniture.

A mitre box, from craft or DIY shops, will enable you to cut accurate right angles and mitres on small pieces, such as door frames, etc (X-acto make a mitre-block designed to work with their razor-toothed saw.) A metal rule, from DIY shops, provides a straight edge for cutting and you will need an ordinary ruler for measuring. A ruler which shows measurements in $\frac{1}{12}$in is the most useful for working in $\frac{1}{12}$ scale. You will also need a well-sharpened HB pencil for marking out and a set square, from DIY shops, for accurately marking and checking right angles. The engineers' set square, available in small sizes, is ideal and although it is a little expensive, is worth the investment.

You will also need a selection of abrasive papers, including fine- and medium-grade sandpaper, and silicon carbide papers, including 280- and 320-grit. These are available from Hobby's (see Magazines, p175). For all furniture-making, we recommend white PVA woodworking glue, eg Evostick Resin W, which is available from DIY shops.

To hold the pieces as you are gluing furniture, you will need a few small cramps. Two 3in cramps and two lighter, $1\frac{1}{2}$in cramps will be sufficient, with several small, strong elastic bands. Hobby's have a good selection of cramps and all of the other tools mentioned here if you cannot find them locally.

Equipped with just these basic tools, the novice could make the furniture projects described in Chapters 2, 4, 5 and 8.

MORE TOOLS · As your interest and ability develop, you will want more tools to expand your scope. Although it is possible to make beautiful furniture with little more than a craft knife, the right tools make the job simpler, quicker and usually produce better results. Good tools are not cheap, but buying the best you can afford is a wise investment, as, taken care of, they will last a lifetime and balanced against the cost of craftsman-made miniatures, the expense is justified.

A set of needle and riffler files will make cleaning up and shaping curved edges and awkward places much easier. The needle files are approximately 5in long and come in a variety of shapes. The half-round, flat and round patterns are the most useful. Riffler files, which are expensive, are also about 5in long and have shaped cutting-edges at both ends. These edges are designed to file irregular shapes such as mouldings.

A small plane, such as the Stanley 7in block plane, will enable you to plane wood to the exact thickness you require and smooth surfaces and edges to a good finish. The block plane has the blade set to a shallower angle than the larger bench plane, so is more appropriate for miniature work.

A fret-saw is essential for tackling anything with curves or cut-outs. The best general-purpose fret-saw is one with a 12in throat. Blades are available in a variety of sizes of which sizes 0/2 to 4 are the most useful. We recommend the Eclipse fret-saw and suggest that the beginner might practise with some scrap wood. For fine work, a fret-saw table (Fig 6) is essential. At first, this tool might seem cumbersome, but used with the right blade, it will cut the finest designs.

Fig 6 THE FRET-SAW TABLE

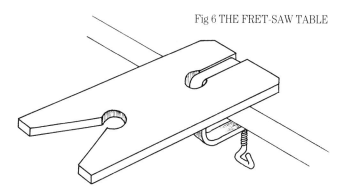

A ¼in chisel is useful for building rather than furniture-making, but a set of miniature chisels has a variety of uses in furniture-making. These chisels are expensive, but a very adequate alternative can be made from watchmaker's screwdrivers, honed to a sharp edge on an oilstone. A set of watchmaker's screwdrivers with blades from ⅛in downwards (and an oil-stone) can be bought in most DIY shops at little cost.

Plate 1 HAND AND POWER TOOLS FOR MAKING MINIATURE FURNITURE

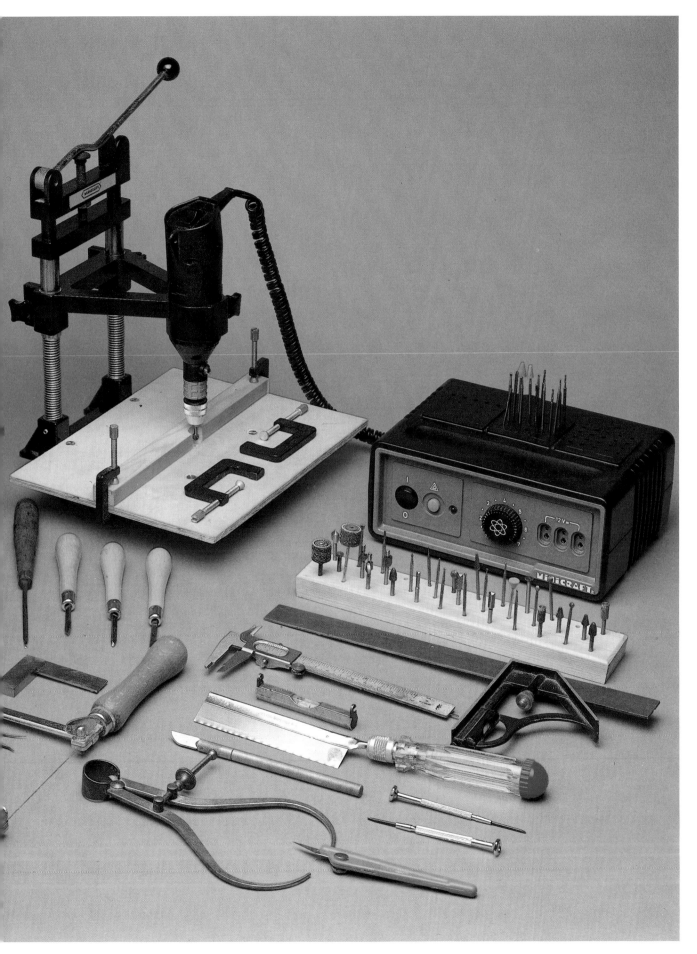

A small brass spirit-level is extremely useful for checking that any flat surface – eg, tabletop or shelf – is level.

A combination square combines a metal rule with a device for measuring right angles and 45° angles. It is particularly useful for marking out and checking the accuracy of furniture pieces during construction.

Calipers are used for measuring thickness – eg, for checking the thickness of a piece of wood – or for comparing the diameter of one piece of turning with another. Two types are available – the vernier type and bow-spring calipers. It is useful to have both types to cover all requirements.

Dividers are used to transfer measurements and are more accurate than measuring directly onto the wood with a ruler. All the tools discussed in this section are available from Hobby's if you cannot find them locally.

POWER TOOLS · Up to this point, we have discussed only hand tools, but eventually any serious miniature furniture-maker will begin to think about power tools. Power tools serve two functions; first, they extend the range of techniques possible to the miniaturist and secondly, they perform tasks which are difficult or time-consuming done by hand. As miniatures become an increasingly more popular hobby, the ranges of power tools available grow, some reasonably priced and others very expensive. We looked for a range of tools that would perform the various functions we required, that were readily available, efficient and reasonably priced. After some research, we chose the Minicraft range from Black & Decker. We have found them to be excellent and recommend them with confidence. Obviously, power tools are not cheap, but as the Minicraft tools are all based on a 12-volt system, once you have bought the transformer, the tools may be bought one at a time as your budget allows. It is best to buy the transformer with variable speed control – it is more expensive than the standard transformer, but will give far more flexibility to the tools.

The most useful tool is probably the Buffalo drill. This, together with an assortment of drill bits, shapers, buffers

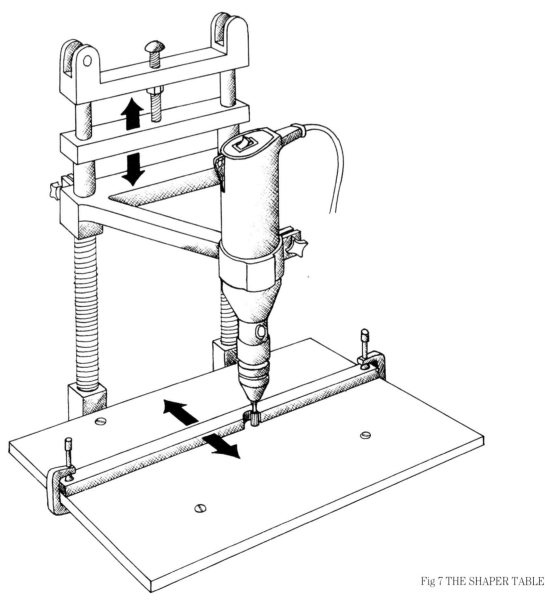

Fig 7 THE SHAPER TABLE

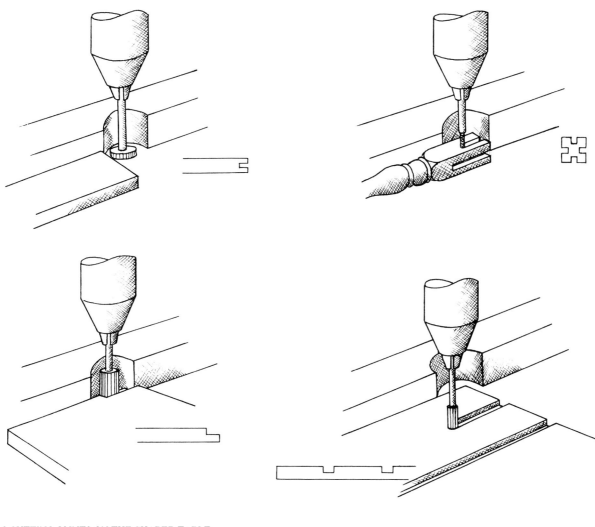

Fig 8 CUTTING JOINTS ON THE SHAPER TABLE

and sanders, will drill holes and shape and polish wood.

The drill press is a device for holding the drill firmly in a vertical position and its main purpose is to ensure accurate drilling. However, the drill and drill press, with minor adjustments, can be used as a shaper table which will considerably extend the range of functions. The shaper table we use is set up in the following way: a piece of ¼in plywood is cut 10 x 8in and fixed to the top of the drill press plate with screws (as shown in Plate 1). A straight guide fence is cut, 1 x ½in, and fitted to the table with clamps. The shaft, used to depress the drill, is removed and replaced with a bolt. The nut is fixed to the bolt so that by turning the nut, the drill can be held rigidly in the chosen position. By using various cutters and router bits in the drill and by adjusting the guide fence, the tool can be used to cut curved mouldings such as door frames and mortice and tenon joints on furniture (see Figs 7, 8 and 9). A variety of accessories is available to fit the drill, of which the most useful are an assortment of drill bits and an assortment of shapers and router bits that are used for carving and shaping wood.

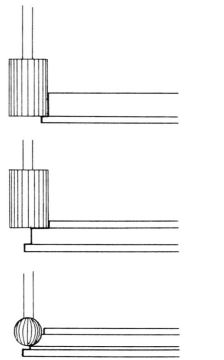

Fig 9 CUTTING A DECORATIVE EDGE ON THE SHAPER TABLE

17

Also useful are variously shaped sanding attachments – including a drum sander and an orbital sander which, while they will not replace hand sanding, will shape a curved surface quickly. Soft fibre buffers fitted to the drill are used to buff furniture with wax polish to a fine finish – a great deal faster than hand-polishing.

A small circular table-saw will cut timber to a maximum depth of 5mm. This saves hours of laborious hand-cutting and gives an accurate finish. While it is not an essential tool because wood can be cut by hand, it is a time-saving and useful accessory.

Minicraft also supply other tools which save time and effort, although those described here are the ones we have found most useful.

The most expensive piece of equipment in our workshop is the lathe. This is, however, an essential item for making any piece of furniture which includes turning. We use a Micro lathe, which is produced by Peatol Machine Tools Ltd. Although it is made as a metal-turning lathe, it is easily adapted for use with wood and is extremely accurate. Many wood-turning lathes do not provide the degree of accuracy required for miniatures simply because of their size. We found the combination of compact size and accuracy of the Peatol lathe ideally suited to our purpose (see Plate 2).

As a cheaper alternative to the Peatol, if you have the Minicraft drill and press, the Minicraft lathe attachment will produce adequate results.

Lathe-turning tools are difficult to find in the tiny sizes that miniatures require. Even those sold as miniature-turning tools are too clumsy for a chair leg 1½in long. We have made our own tools from a set of ordinary small woodworking chisels that were bought cheaply in the local market and ground to shape on a grindstone. The best set of commercial tools are those made by Dremel. Although the Dremel lathe does not have the range and accuracy of more expensive models, it is an acceptable alternative for anyone with a limited budget.

SAFETY · All tools are potentially dangerous and should therefore be stored carefully, completely out of the reach of children. Even something as simple as a craft knife in a child's hands can cause serious harm.

The following rules are offered as a guideline:

1 When using tools, especially power tools, ensure that you are properly dressed. Do not wear loose clothing, such as sleeves, ties, etc. Tie long hair back. Wear safety glasses.
2 Check power plugs regularly. Do not overload sockets: use one plug only per socket. Ensure that electric leads are well away from the work area. (Consider installing a circuit breaker.) Never leave a power tool running and unattended. Unplug tools when they are not being used (even for a few minutes).
3 Never use tools, especially power tools, when you are tired, unwell or have been drinking alcohol.
4 Tidy up the work area regularly. Have a place for each tool and keep each tool in that place. Take care of your tools and check them regularly. Make sure that cutting tools are kept sharp – a blunt tool needs more pressure to use and increases the risk that the tool might slip.
5 Ensure that you work in adequate light – normal domestic lighting is not sufficient. Spot-lights are good when strong daylight is not available.
6 Make sure that everyone in your household understands the rules.

Provided that you follow these basic rules, your tools will give you good service and your miniature-making will be safe and enjoyable.

MATERIALS · The most easily available woods for furniture-making are obeche and basswood which can be bought at most craft and model shops in sheets of various thicknesses, 3in wide x 3ft long. These are white woods, which are easily worked and can be finished to represent a variety of timbers. These are probably the best choice for the beginner. Select carefully the pieces you buy as the pattern of the grain, particularly on obeche, varies considerably from piece to piece. Choose those with a fine grain in 1/16in, 3/32in and 1/8in thicknesses. Check also that the pieces you buy are flat and straight, not warped. In the same place you will find a selection of obeche or basswood strips and dowelling. These strips are inexpensive and it is useful to have a good selection to hand – the most useful will probably be 1/4in and 1/2in strips and 1/8in and 1/16in square strips. Dowelling, in 1/8in and 1/16in diameter, is also useful.

Because bass- and obeche wood are inexpensive and easy to work with, they are the ideal choice for the beginner, but as your confidence and ability grow, you will want to use more authentic woods. Mahogany-stained obeche wood does not look as 'real' as mahogany, and once your furniture making has reached a certain standard, it is well worth spending a little more on materials to buy 'real' wood. Mahogany, walnut and spruce are readily available from most craft and model shops in similar sized sheets. Again, select with care, paying particular attention to the grain as tiny furniture pieces need the smallest possible grain to look convincing.

The best source of supply for wood is old furniture because the wood obtained from old furniture is thoroughly seasoned and stable. Junk shops, antique dealers and furniture restorers all have off-cuts of old woods and are usually prepared to give or sell pieces they do not need. These pieces will, of course, need to be sawn into usable thicknesses and for this you will need a circular saw. If you do not have access to a circular saw, try a local cabinetmaker (see Yellow Pages) who may be willing to saw it for you. This is the type of wood we use for our own furniture.

If you are fortunate enough to have a specialist timber merchant in your area, ask for small off-cuts of wood – these will need to be sawn to the thickness you need.

Old furniture and specialist timber merchants will extend the range of woods available to include pine, oak, cherry, yew, satin walnut (banana wood) and beech, etc.

Wood sawn on a circular saw will need planing to a perfectly smooth finish before it can be used.

Timber is available from various mail-order sources, but we do not recommend buying it this way. It is far better to select your own pieces than to rely on someone else's choice and risk disappointment.

CUTTING · Some timbers will need to be planed to the correct thickness before use and this must be done following the grain of the wood (Fig 10). A bench hook is a useful device for holding the small pieces of timber that are used – Fig 11 shows a typical example. Even planing small pieces of wood requires some practice to achieve a perfectly flat surface – so practise first on scrap wood.

Marking out the furniture pieces on the wood is best done with a very sharp HB pencil, although on some dark woods it is better to score a line with a craft knife. The furniture plans in the book are all drawn full size and you should transfer them to your wood using a good pair of dividers, a ruler and an engineer's set square.

To mark out a rectangular piece, prepare one straight edge on the timber. This is best done using the bench hook and the small block plane (see Fig 9). This will ensure that the edge is not only straight but is at right angles to the surface.

Using the engineer's square against this edge, mark the piece required (Fig 12). Using the dividers, measure the width of the piece to be cut along these lines. Mark the other edge using the pencil and metal rule.

Cuts made across the grain must be on the drawn line as it is not practicable to plane across the end grain. Use the bench hook to support the piece and cut with a fine razor-tooth saw. Cuts along the grain are best made slightly proud of the drawn line and planed to the line, using the bench hook as described.

These notes apply when cutting virtually every rectangular piece, whether it be a shelf, a table-top, a door, etc.

JOINTING · Three basic types of jointing have been used in the projects.

The simplest method is the butt joint. This is a joint whereby one straight edge is glued directly against another. It relies solely on the strength of the glue and makes a simple and relatively efficient joint (Fig 13a).

The second method is the pegged joint. This is similar to the butt joint but has the added strength of small pegs which fit into holes drilled in both pieces. Pegged joints may be simply made by first assembling a butt joint and then drilling holes $\frac{1}{16}$in in diameter through both pieces to receive dowelling pegs which are glued in place. The pegs are trimmed flush with the surface and are masked by the final finish (Fig 13b). A neater method of peg jointing, and one which gives the pieces some support during assembly, is made by fitting the pegs into the surfaces to be glued and drilling the receiving holes into, but not through, the wood. With this method, the pegs are completely concealed, but it does require very accurate marking for the receiving holes (Figs 13c and d).

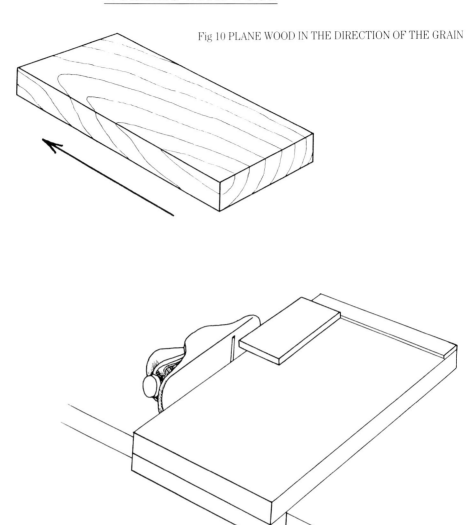

Fig 10 PLANE WOOD IN THE DIRECTION OF THE GRAIN

Fig 11 USING THE BENCH HOOK AND PLANE TO PREPARE TIMBER

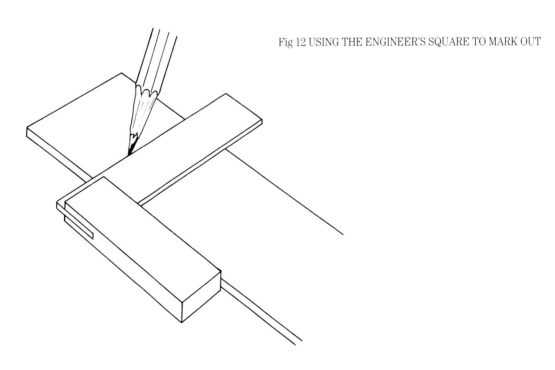

Fig 12 USING THE ENGINEER'S SQUARE TO MARK OUT

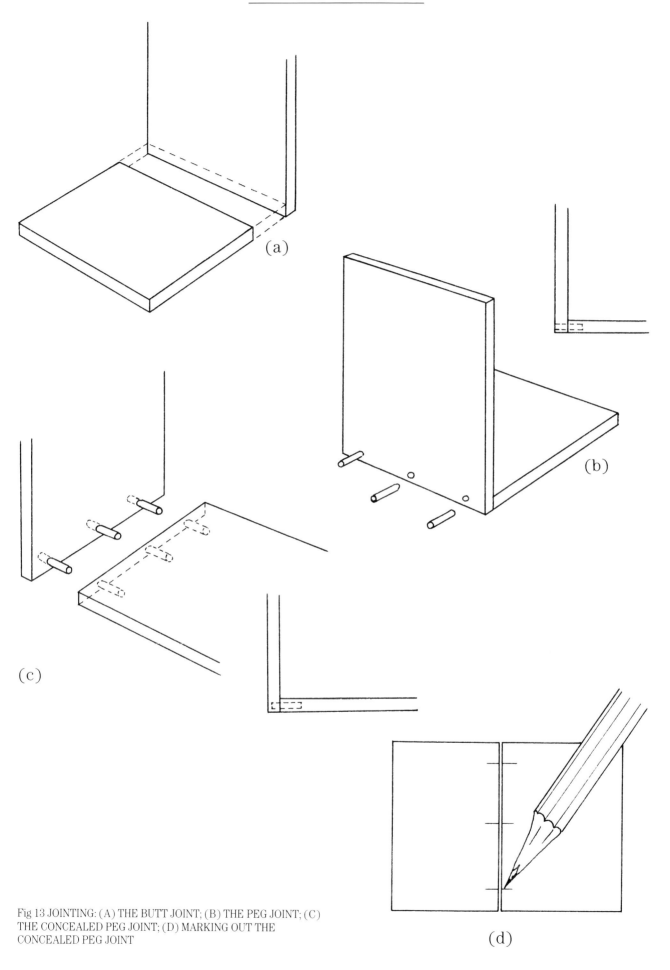

Fig 13 JOINTING: (A) THE BUTT JOINT; (B) THE PEG JOINT; (C)
THE CONCEALED PEG JOINT; (D) MARKING OUT THE
CONCEALED PEG JOINT

The most authentic method of jointing – and the strongest – is a combination of rabbet and dado joints, and mortise and tenon joints. In this method, the two pieces of wood are interlocked in various ways. The main advantage of this type of joint is that, although they are more difficult to cut, when they are cut accurately, assembly is much simpler as the pieces are virtually self-supporting – even without glue – and the finished joints are very strong. The dado joint consists of a recess cut into one piece which receives the edge of the interlocking piece – as in a shelf set into the sides of a bookcase. The rabbet joint is similar, but is used on the carcase of a piece of furniture – for example, on the back of a chest of drawers (Figs 14 and 15). Both of these joints can be cut using a craft knife and metal rule to mark them out and a small watchmaker's 'chisel' for cutting, but are more easily done using the shaper table described under Power Tools on p17. You might practise first with scrap wood.

The mortise and tenon joint is used mainly for fixing rails such as those on tables – where the rail is fitted into the table legs. Fig 16 shows the proportions used in this joint. These joints can be cut using a small watchmaker's 'chisel', but again are more easily produced on a shaper table.

Throughout the book, the joints that have been used for each piece of furniture are shown in the assembly drawings and are described in the text. If you wish to use a simple butt joint rather than the more difficult joints, most pieces will adapt, but allowance must be made in measuring to eliminate the extra wood required for the joint described.

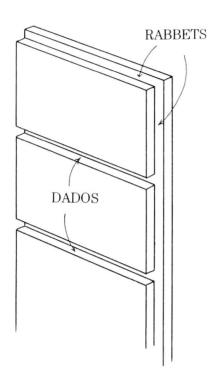

RABBETS

DADOS

Fig 14 RABBETS AND DADOS CUT TO RECEIVE SHELVES, ETC

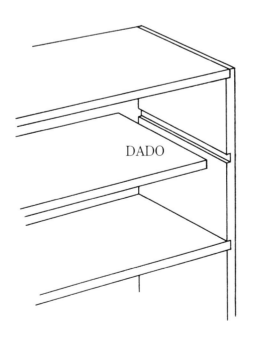

DADO

Fig 15 CARCASE CONSTRUCTION USING RABBET AND DADO JOINTS

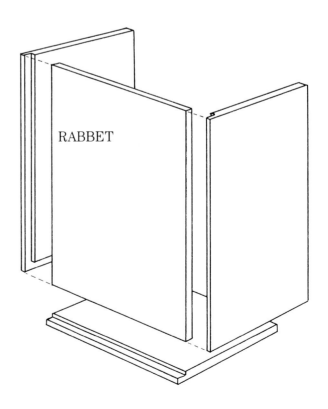

RABBET

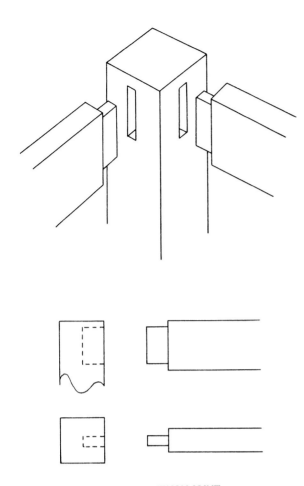

Fig 16 TYPICAL MORTISE AND TENON JOINT

MAKING DRAWERS · Two methods of drawer construction have been used – one simple, the other more authentic. Either method may be used for any of the projects in the book.

Method 1 Cut the drawer front to fit the drawer opening, allowing a fraction of clearance so that the drawer will open and close easily. Cut the drawer bottom from ³/₃₂in thick wood, the same width as the drawer front and as deep as required (Fig 17a). Glue the bottom behind the drawer front, ensuring that you make a perfect right angle (Fig 18). Cut the sides and back from ¹/₁₆in thick wood and glue them onto the base to complete the drawer. If necessary, sand the top edges of the drawer sides and back so that the drawer fits well.

Method 2 The drawer is constructed by rebating the sides into the front and the back into the sides. The bottom is fitted into a groove which has been cut to accommodate it in the sides, front and back. Cut the drawer front in ³/₃₂in thick wood to fit the drawer opening, allowing a fraction of clearance. Cut rabbets at each end of the drawer front to accommodate the sides. Measure the required depth of the drawer and cut the sides from ¹/₁₆in thick wood so that the overall length, including the drawer front, fits this depth. Cut rabbets in the drawer sides to accommodate the back. Cut the back to fit. Before assembly, cut a ¹/₃₂in groove as close as possible to the lower edge of each piece to accommodate the base. This groove should be cut to the same depth as the

(a)

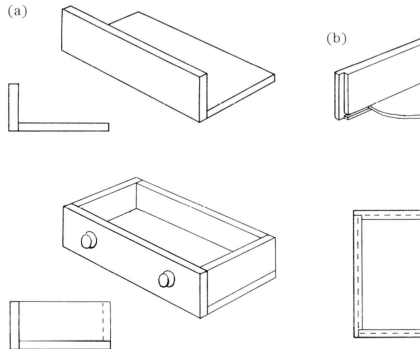

(b)

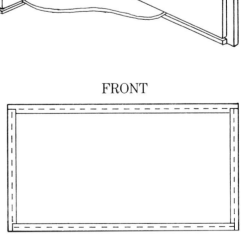

FRONT

FRONT

Fig 17 MAKING DRAWERS: (A) SIMPLE DRAWER
CONSTRUCTION; (B) AUTHENTIC DRAWER CONSTRUCTION

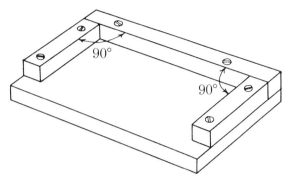

Fig 18 SIMPLE JIG USED TO CHECK RIGHT ANGLES

rabbets. Glue the sides to the front, ensuring that these are at perfect right angles, and allow the glue to dry. Cut the base from ⅛in thick plywood to fit into the prepared grooves, allowing a slight overhang to fit into the groove which has been cut in the drawer back (Fig 17b). Glue the back in place to complete the drawer.

This second method of drawer construction is only practicable if you have a shaper table – but given that, it is easier to do than to describe!

TURNING · Whichever type of lathe you choose, the method of holding the wood in the headstock must be considered. Round-section wood is best held in an adjustable 'Jacob's' chuck (the type found on most electric drills), as this is smaller and less daunting then the usual three-jaw chuck. It allows very small turnings to be made without the risk of skinning your knuckles. Square-section wood, such as is required for table legs, etc, is best held with a two- or four-prong driver. The one we use is

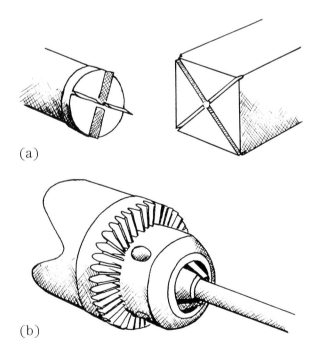

(a)

(b)

Fig 19 LATHE CHUCKS: (A) THE FOUR-PRONGED CHUCK; (B) THE 'JACOB'S' CHUCK

from an old Dremel lathe and is small enough to be held in a ½in 'Jacob's' chuck (see Fig 19).

To make a turning, first draw the pattern on paper (see Fig 20). Turn the wood to a diameter slightly larger than the largest part of the finished turning. Mark the main divisions of the turning on the blank with a sharp pencil. Fig 21 shows how the variously shaped chisels will cut different features.

Work slowly, removing a little wood at a time and checking regularly with the bow-spring calipers that the diameters conform to the pattern. When the turning is complete, use a needle file where necessary to smooth the curves and a pointed chisel (skew chisel) to define the undercuts sharply. Remove the tool rest and, with the lathe running, lightly sand with very fine abrasive paper.

If a number of turnings are required from the same pattern, repeat the above operation, transferring measurements from the first turning with dividers, and checking the diameters frequently with bow-spring calipers.

We would suggest to the beginner that while turning one piece is relatively straightforward, it is more difficult to produce a set of four perfectly matched turnings. It is best, therefore, to turn a simple pattern and aim to match it, rather than try something too elaborate.

When finishing the turning, stain can be applied while the piece is on the lathe.

It is not possible in a book of this type to give detailed instructions on how to use a lathe. The beginner will find it helpful to refer to a good book on basic wood-turning techniques and to practise and experiment. The techniques used for miniature turning are basically the same as those used for life-sized projects.

FINISHING · Finishing is one of the most important processes in making miniature furniture. However well made the piece is, it will not look convincing unless the finish is good.

Although the various parts of a piece of furniture will have been sanded thoroughly before assembly, the finished piece must be given a final sanding with 280-grit and then 320-grit abrasive paper so that it feels thoroughly smooth to the touch. Always sand following the grain of the wood and on flat surfaces use the abrasive paper wrapped around a small block to avoid rounding any edges. Remove all traces of dust.

STAINING · Any wood may be stained to colour it, as with obeche, or to enhance its colour, as with mahogany. Choose any good brand of spirit-based wood stain, such as Rustins or Blackfriars. These stains are available in a range of colours from DIY shops and can be mixed or thinned with white spirit to produce any colour you want.

Wood stain will not penetrate wood glue, so during assembly, any glue leakage must be removed with a damp cloth. For this reason, small pieces are often better stained before assembly. The stain may be applied either with an artist's paint-brush or with a piece of lint-free cloth. Brush or wipe it on in the direction of the grain. Use

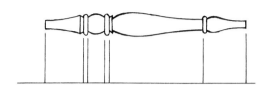

Fig 20 MARKING OUT THE MAIN DIVISIONS FROM A PATTERN

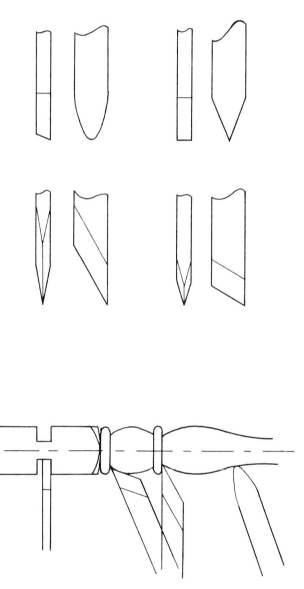

Fig 21 BASIC WOOD-TURNING CHISEL SHAPES AND THEIR USES

the stain sparingly as a second coat may be applied when the first is dry to intensify the colour. Apply stain with a cloth as it is easier to control the colour with the lighter application that a cloth, rather than a brush, produces.

Stained pieces may be rubbed down with 320-grit paper to simulate wear on edges, foot-rests, etc where such would naturally colour. Similarly, a darker coat of stain may be applied in corners, etc to simulate an appearance of ageing. Do be careful not to overdo this 'ageing' though, as in this small scale, subtlety is much more effective.

Stained pieces must be allowed to dry thoroughly – a process which varies from wood to wood. Obeche wood will dry overnight, but the less absorbent yew can take several days. When the stain is thoroughly dry to the touch, it is ready for finishing. If necessary, gently sand the piece with 320-grit paper and remove all traces of dust.

If you are making fine miniatures in open-grained wood such as mahogany, it is worth the effort required to fill the open grain before polishing. This is done with a grain filler (not to be confused with plastic wood), which is available from some DIY shops. The filler is a paste which is worked into the wood, across the grain, with a piece of cloth. Allow a few minutes for the filler to dry and wipe off the excess with a rough cloth, working along the grain. It may be necessary to apply a second coat. When the grain is filled and the filler is thoroughly dry, sand the piece with 320-grit paper to a perfect smoothness.

POLISHING · Polyurethane varnish may be used to finish miniature furniture, but the deeper, more subtle sheen of French polish is more realistic. However, if you prefer to use varnish, we suggest a satin or matt finish rather than gloss and the varnish must be thinned at least 50 per cent with white spirit. The method for varnish is the same as that which follows for French polishing.

French polish is available in three types, which are determined by the colour of the varnish. Buy the 'clear' or 'white' type of French polish as this changes the colour of the wood less than the other types. French polish should be thinned 25 to 30 per cent with methylated spirit (denatured alcohol). It can be applied by brush, but it is essential that a top-quality artist's brush, preferably sable, be used. Alternatively, prepare a rubber by wrapping a piece of cotton cloth around a small pad of cotton-wool. The polish is applied sparingly to the cotton-wool and seeps through the cloth as the rubber is used. Whichever method you use, aim for a thin, even coat of polish. The polish will become tacky almost immediately, so work with quick, even strokes along the grain and allow it to dry. Do not attempt to patch in missed areas because any areas which have been missed will be covered in subsequent coats. The first coat will dry quickly and within five minutes a second coat can be applied. Allow this second coat to harden overnight, then sand with a worn piece of 320-grit paper and remove all traces of dust. The finish at this stage may look very patchy. Repeat the polishing process, sanding again if necessary, until a deep shine is achieved. This can take several days and should not be rushed. Good results need patience.

French polishing gives the piece a deep shine which may not be appropriate for all furniture. If you prefer a soft sheen, rather than a shine, for example on kitchen furniture, achieve a good French polished finish as described, then sand lightly with used 320-grit paper until the bright shine disappears. Apply a thin coat of good quality beeswax polish and buff to a sheen. Repeat applications of wax polish until the effect you want is achieved.

PAINTING · If you wish to paint furniture, a smoothly sanded surface is essential before you begin. If the wood has an open grain, this will show through paint, so must be filled first. Apply a coat of sanding sealer (available from craft and model shops) with a paint-brush, allow it to dry, then sand with 320-grit paper. Repeat the process until the grain is filled. We recommend Humbrol enamel paints for furniture – household emulsion or gloss paints do not give satisfactory results. Paint the piece with an undercoat of matt paint, allow to dry thoroughly, then sand with 320-grit paper until it is perfectly smooth, then remove all traces of dust. Apply a coat of matt or gloss paint in the chosen colour, allow it to dry and sand lightly. Apply a final coat and allow it to dry. Apply thin coats of paint, using a good quality artist's paint-brush. Humbrol enamel colours can be mixed to make any shade you choose and thinned with white spirit if necessary. The painted finish may be 'aged' by sanding gently with 320-grit paper in areas where wear would naturally occur. When 'ageing' painted pieces, a light touch is needed so that the 'worn' area blends naturally and does not look as though the paint has simply chipped off. Do not overdo the ageing process as subtlety is more effective.

2
SHOEBOX ROOMS

Shoebox rooms are made very simply in thick cardboard and decorated with wrapping-paper and fabric scraps. The rooms are designed to be sturdy enough for children to play with. One side lets down to extend the floor of the room and, when play is over, the box holds everything safe and tidily. The simple furniture pieces are made of stained or painted obeche wood and padded cardboard. Even the absolute beginner should find no difficulty in making the boxes and their contents.

TO MAKE A SHOEBOX

You will need one large sheet of ⅛in thick art cardboard – cardboard boxes, etc will not produce good results – a craft knife and metal ruler, UHU glue and 1in wide masking-tape. To decorate the box, you will need two sheets of wrapping-paper with a small pattern, a sheet of brown parcel wrapping-paper and wallpaper paste. The box is tied with 2yd of wide satin ribbon.

To make the box, cut one base, two sides and two ends, using a craft knife and metal ruler (see Fig 22a). See the assembly diagram shown in Fig 22b and try the pieces in place, checking that they fit well. Assemble the pieces, using UHU glue along the edges and masking-tape over the joins. Assemble the base inside the two ends and one side. Turn the box over onto its open top, fit the second side in place – without glue – and tape the second side to the base only. Turn the box back onto its base and let the second side down flat. There is a gap between the base and the side which allows the side to lie flat. Brush a little talcum powder into this gap to prevent the tape from sticking in it, and tape along the join to cover the gap on the inside (Fig 22b). The second side is now 'hinged' and should open and close freely.

To make the lid, draw around the base of the box to obtain the correct size for the top of the lid. Cut 1½in wide strips of card to fit around the edges of the top to make the sides. Glue and tape the top inside the sides. Check that the lid fits well, but not tightly.

Cover the box and the lid with small-patterned wrapping-paper, pasted with wallpaper paste. You may prefer to use a different pattern (or dolls' house wallpaper – see list of stockists, pp175-9) for the inside 'walls' of the box. Cut a piece of brown parcel wrapping-paper to fit the base and let-down side, and paste it in to represent the floor. Allow the papered box to dry thoroughly. It is important to paper both the outside and the inside of the box at the same time to minimise the risk of warping. It may be necessary to press the base and let-down side under a heavy weight as it dries if it shows a tendency to warp.

SITTING-ROOM

CHIMNEY-BREAST · The chimney-breast is a 4in wide piece of balsa wood, ½in thick, cut to fit the height of the box. The balsa wood is covered in pasted wrapping-paper like a parcel and, when dry, is glued to the centre of the back wall with UHU glue (Fig 23).

FIREPLACE · The fireplace is made from a 3in square block of balsa wood ⅜in thick and faced with ⅛in thick obeche wood. Cut the square opening (marked on the diagram with dotted lines) in the balsa block. Face the sides of the block with obeche wood. Cut the front pillars in obeche and glue them in place. Cut the lintel to fit between the pillars, and glue. Cut a piece of thin, stiff cardboard to fit inside the lintel and pillars, and cut the arched opening as shown on the diagram. Glue the cardboard in place. Trim the fireplace with small pieces of picture-frame moulding (dolls' house skirting-board, etc) glued in place. Cut the mantelshelf as required and glue to the top of the fireplace. Paint the interior of the fireplace matt black and the surround as required – Humbrol enamel gloss paint in ivory was used in the example. Glue a magazine cut-out of a burning fire to the back of the fireplace and glue the fireplace to the chimney-breast. Make a hearth from a small piece of tile-effect paper.

CARPET · The carpet may be made of almost any plain or printed fabric – felt, needlecord and velvet are particularly suitable. We have used a remnant of Dralon furnishing velvet. Lightweight iron-on Vilene, ironed onto the back of the fabric before cutting, will prevent the edges from fraying. Cut the carpet to fit just inside the edges of the floor, shaping around the chimney-breast and hearth. (You might find it helpful to make a paper pattern before cutting the fabric.) Make sure that you cut

(CONTINUED ON P.30)

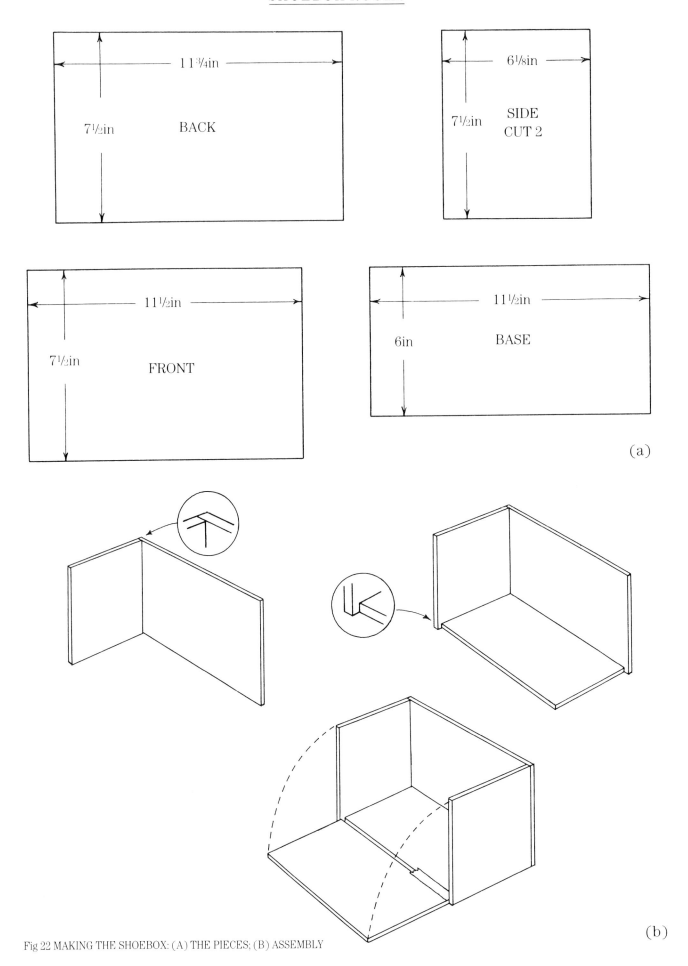

Fig 22 MAKING THE SHOEBOX: (A) THE PIECES; (B) ASSEMBLY

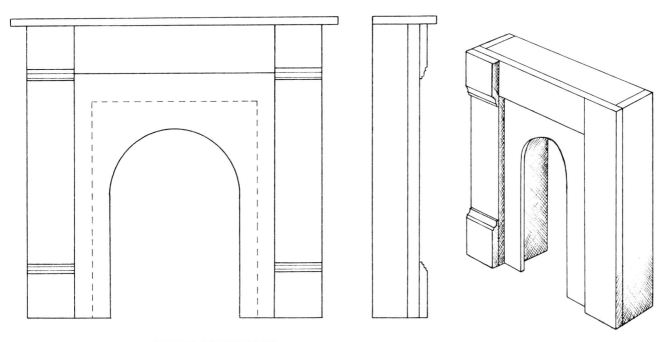

Fig 23 PATTERN AND ASSEMBLY FOR SITTING-ROOM
FIREPLACE

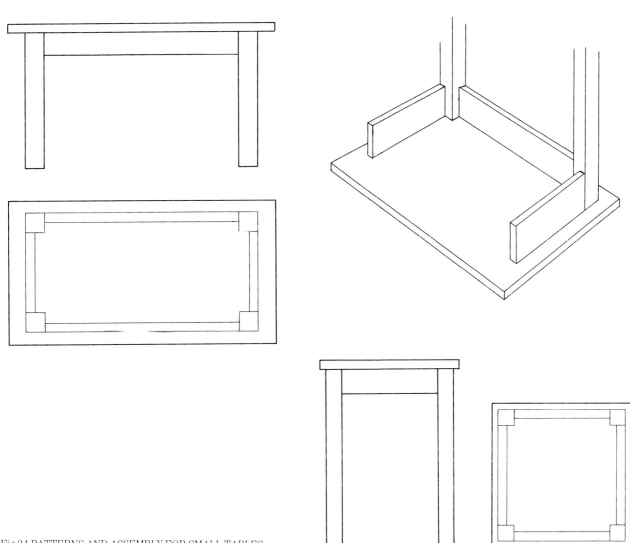

Fig 24 PATTERNS AND ASSEMBLY FOR SMALL TABLES

the fabric squarely on the grain – on Dralon velvet this is simply done along the length by following the ribs of the weave on the back of the fabric. Very pretty rugs and carpets may be made by printing a pattern onto the velvet with felt pens. Do not stick the carpet to the floor as it forms an ugly crease across the centre where the box is closed, but it it is left loose laid, this problem does not arise. The rug shown in the plate opposite is a table-mat from the local department store, but you might also consider commercial dolls'-house rugs.

WOODEN FURNITURE · Read 'Making Furniture' in Chapter 1 for full instructions for cutting, assembling and finishing wooden furniture. The pieces in this chapter are simple to make, but if you wish to adapt the patterns to more authentic methods of construction, assembly instructions can be found in Chapter 1. The furniture is all made in ³/₃₂in thick obeche wood, finished with walnut woodstain and polish, but 'real' wood may be used if you prefer. All patterns are drawn full size.

TABLES · Patterns are given for two small tables – the method of construction is the same for both (Fig 24).
    Cut four legs, four friezes and a top from the pattern. Check that the legs are all exactly the same length and that the pairs of friezes are a perfect match. Assemble one pair of legs, butted and glued to either side of one frieze (Fig 24). When this is dry, glue to the table-top. Glue the side friezes to the top, butted to the legs. Assemble the second pair of legs and last frieze and, when dry, butt to the side friezes. Sand, stain and polish the piece as required.

Plate 3 THE SHOEBOX SITTING-ROOM

SMALL STORAGE UNIT · Cut two sides, one back, one shelf and one top. Cut ³⁄₂in grooves in both side pieces, marking out with a craft knife and metal rule, and cutting with a watchmaker's 'chisel'. (If you do not have this tool, the shelf may be cut to butt between the sides.) Glue the back to one side. Glue the shelf to the back and side. Glue the second side in place. Glue the top in place. Sand, stain and polish as required.

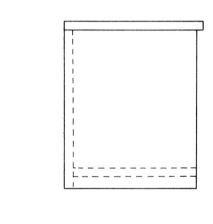

LARGE STORAGE UNIT · The large unit is made in two pieces, as a cupboard and a book-shelf, assembled separately and glued together.

To make the cupboard (Fig 26), cut two sides, a back, a base and a top. Glue the back to one side. Glue the base to the back and side. Glue the second side in place. The doors are hinged with dressmaker's pins. Cut the doors to fit snugly into the front. Sand the hinged edges of the doors slightly rounded so that they will swing freely. Bore a fine hole with a dressmaker's pin into the top and bottom corners of the doors. Bore the hole as close as possible to the edge, taking care to work gently so that you do not split the wood. Push pins into the holes and snip off to leave approximately ³⁄₂in protruding. Reverse the pins so that the pointed ends now protrude. Position the doors on the front of the cupboard and bore holes in the base to receive the pins. Fit the top of the cupboard, mark and bore the pin holes, check that the doors swing freely, trim if necessary, then glue the top in place.

To make the shelf unit, cut two sides, one back, a top and two shelves. Glue the back to one side. Glue the two shelves to the back and side. Fit and glue the second side. Glue the top in place.

Glue the shelf unit to the top of the cupboard, sand, stain and polish as required.

Escutcheon pins (available from DIY shops) have been used for door handles. You may prefer to use miniature handles from one of the specialist suppliers. Drill holes into the doors to receive the handles, snip the pins to the required length and glue them into the holes with UHU or similar glue.

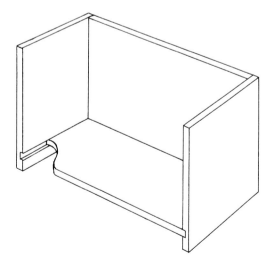

Fig 25 PATTERN AND ASSEMBLY FOR SMALL STORAGE UNIT

Fig 26 PATTERN AND ASSEMBLY FOR LARGE STORAGE UNIT

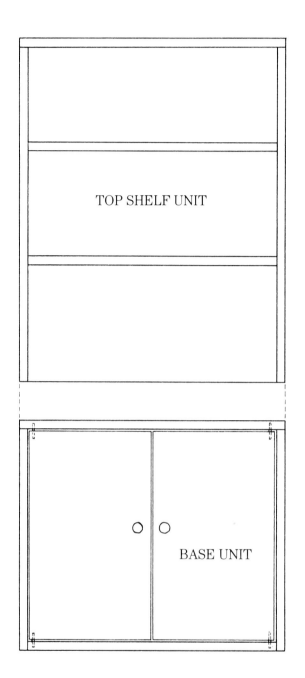

TOP SHELF UNIT

BASE UNIT

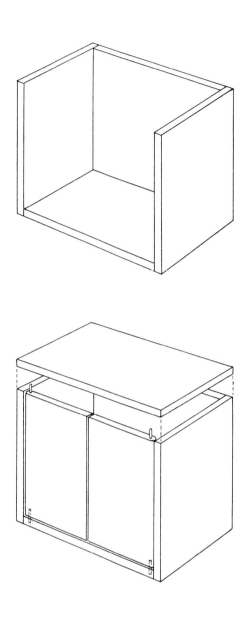

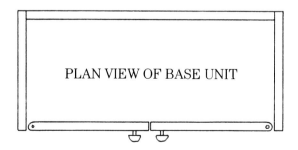

PLAN VIEW OF BASE UNIT

Fig 27 PATTERN FOR UPHOLSTERED CHAIR AND SOFA

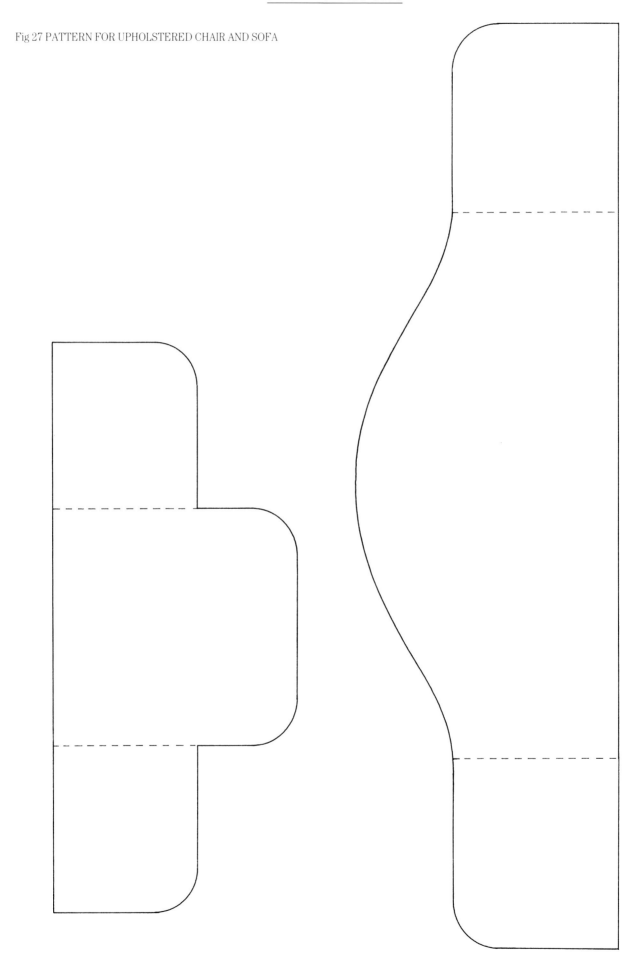

UPHOLSTERED FURNITURE · The simple upholstered furniture in this chapter is made of cardboard, padded with foam and covered with fabric. The cardboard should be good quality art card, firm, but not too thick – cereal packets, etc are too flimsy. The foam padding should be about ¼in thick and this is readily available in sheets – we buy it from the local market. Fabric for covers should be carefully chosen – avoid anything thick, stretchy or with a large pattern. Cotton fabrics are best. Village Fabrics (see list of stockists, p176) sell an enormous range of cottons in plain colours and tiny patterns. Several of their fabrics in co-ordinating colours and patterns have been used to make the sofa, chairs and cushions.

To make a chair or sofa, the method is the same (see Fig 27). Cut the pattern twice in cardboard. Score the vertical lines marked on the pattern with a scissor blade and bend the arms on both pieces forward. Draw the pattern onto a doubled thickness of fabric, squarely on the grain, and cut the fabric covers ½in larger all around than the drawn pattern line. Draw the pattern onto the foam and cut one piece ½in larger all around than the drawn pattern line. You should have two card pieces, two fabric pieces and one foam piece.

Glue the foam (with UHU) to the inside of one cardboard piece, rolling the ½in overlap over the edges all the way around and gluing it to the back. Glue the second card piece to the outside of the chair, lining up the bottom edges, so that it fits inside the padding around the arms and back (Fig 28).

Stitch the cover pieces together around the outside edge – right sides facing – using the drawn pattern line as the stitching line and leaving the bottom edge open. Clip the corners and turn through.

Ease the padded card into the cover, working carefully to smooth out any creases and stretching the cover as taut as possible. Turn in the raw edges and slip stitch the lower edge closed. With your fingers, gently roll this slip-stitched edge to the inside of the chair.

The seat of the chair (or sofa) is made of a block of balsa wood, ½in thick, as shown on the bedroom chair and sofa, or of a piece of obeche wood, ⅛in thick, as shown on the sitting-room chairs. The wood is cut to fit snugly inside the back and arms of the chair. Pad the front and top of the seat and cover it in fabric like a parcel, gluing the ends firmly in place.

The seat is glued along the side and back edges and fitted into the chair. Pins, pushed through the chair into the seat, or elastic bands, will hold everything in place until the glue is dry.

Seat-cushions may be made as simple stuffed 'bag' cushions, like the one on the bedroom chair, or cut in foam and covered like a parcel, like the sitting-room chairs. Glue the seat cushion in place.

The underside of the chairs and sofa can be neatened with a piece of felt or carpet tape glued in place and round or square wooden beads will make good feet, glued or pinned with gimp pins under each corner. Small

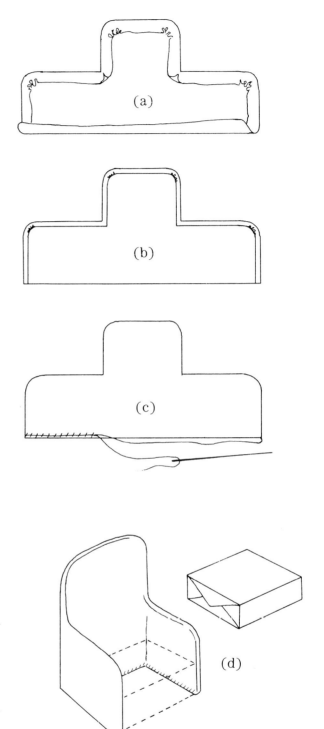

Fig 28 UPHOLSTERED CHAIR OR SOFA ASSEMBLY

stuffed cushions tucked into the corners of the chair or sofa complete it.

These pieces, although simple, are strong and can look very effective if the fabrics are carefully chosen and the work is neat. The choice of fabric and the depth of the seat will make the pattern suitable for a modern or traditional setting.

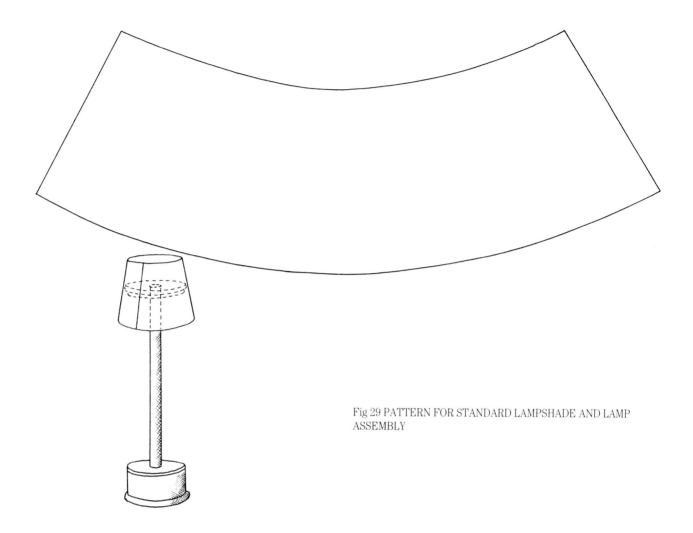

Fig 29 PATTERN FOR STANDARD LAMPSHADE AND LAMP
ASSEMBLY

LAMPS · The standard lamp is made from a cotton-reel, a plastic washer and a felt-pen casing. The shade is cotton fabric, backed with heavyweight iron-on Vilene and trimmed with narrow braid. To make the lamp, saw the cotton-reel through, just below one end (Fig 29). Glue the washer over the cut end of the large piece of cotton-reel. Glue the felt-pen casing into the hole in the washer and cotton-reel. Glue the smaller piece of cotton-reel to the top of the felt-pen casing. Paint this assembly with Humbrol enamel paint and allow to dry. Draw the lampshade pattern on Vilene, iron onto the fabric and cut out. Overlap and glue the seam. Glue narrow braid to the top and lower edges. Glue the outside edge of the top piece of cotton-reel and rest the shade in place. If your lamp is top-heavy, weight the base by filling the hole in the cotton-reel with Plasticine or clay.

The small lamp is made of a broken chess-set pawn, with a small plastic washer to hold the shade in place – in the same way as the standard lamp.

ACCESSORIES · The books on the shelves are made from magazine illustrations, cut out and wrapped around small blocks of wood. The magazines are cut from advertisements for 'next week's issue' showing tiny covers; the pages are typing paper stapled into the covers.

The ornaments are all beads, buttons and tiny shells. There is a large selection of fancy buttons in most haberdashery departments, many of which will make simple ornaments. The plates on the wall are buttons with magazine pictures glued to the centre. The wastepaper basket is a bottle cap (Brut aftershave lotion) trimmed with narrow braid. The pictures are cut from birthday cards, framed with thin wood-strip, mitred at the corners. The clock is simply a shaped block of wood with a cut-out clock face, framed with a brass curtain-ring glued onto the front.

The dog beside the fire is from The Dolls' House (see list of stockists, p176) and instructions for the potted plant (in a toothpaste-cap pot) can be found on p84. Instructions for the silk-ribbon roses are given on p89 and for the fruit arranged in a large glass-button bowl on pp56–7.

The log basket is made of plaited raffia, filled with small twig logs and the poker is a rivet. The miniature carrier-bag has thread handles and is filled with tiny balls of wool, magazine illustration knitting-patterns and pins for knitting-needles. The doll holds a piece of knitting worked on pins.

THE BEDROOM

FURNITURE · (Refer to 'Making Furniture' in Chapter 1 for full instructions for assembling and finishing wooden furniture.) All the bedroom furniture is made from ³⁄₃₂in and ¹⁄₈in obeche wood with a small piece of ¹⁄₄in obeche for the wardrobe. The furniture has been painted with ivory Humbrol enamel paint – a matt undercoat and two gloss topcoats, sanded between each coat.

ARMCHAIR · The armchair (Fig 30) is made in the same way as the chairs in the sitting-room.

TABLE · Cut four legs, four friezes and a top (see Fig 31a). Check that the legs are all exactly the same length and that the pairs of friezes are a perfect match. Assemble one pair of legs, butted and glued to either side of one frieze. When this is dry, glue the legs and frieze to the table-top. Glue the side friezes to the top, butted to the legs. Assemble the second pair of legs and last frieze and, when dry, butt to the side friezes. Sand and paint (or stain and polish) as required.

CHAIR · Cut four legs, a seat, four stretchers and two back rails from the pattern (Fig 31b). Glue the two back rails between the back legs. Dry-fit the seat in place to hold the back legs in position as the glue dries. Glue the seat to the back legs at right angles and allow the assembly to dry thoroughly. Glue the front legs in place and allow to dry. Glue the ends of the stretchers and ease them gently into place, removing any glue seepage. Sand and paint as required.

BED · Cut the pieces shown in Fig 32 and cut a piece of ¹⁄₈in obeche wood, 6in long for the base. Glue the long side rails to the base. To assemble the headboard, glue the three slats between the top and bottom rails and allow to dry thoroughly. Glue this assembly between the legs. Assemble the footboard by gluing the rails between the legs. Glue the head- and footboard assemblies to the base. Rest the bed on one side until the glue is dry so that the base does not slip out of place. Sand and paint as required.

CHEST OF DRAWERS · To build the carcase of the chest-of-drawers, cut two sides, a back and four drawer dividers (Fig 33). Glue the back to one side. Glue the four dividers to the back and side. Glue the second side in place. Cut the top from the pattern, chamfer the edges of the sides and front and glue to the top of the carcase, lining up the back edges. Cut the base, chamfer the side and front top edges and glue in place, lining up the back edges. To make the drawers, see the instructions given in 'Making Furniture' in Chapter 1, and use the simpler, first method described. Escutcheon pins, glued into holes drilled in the drawer fronts, have been used for the handles. Sand and paint the carcase exterior and the drawer fronts as required.

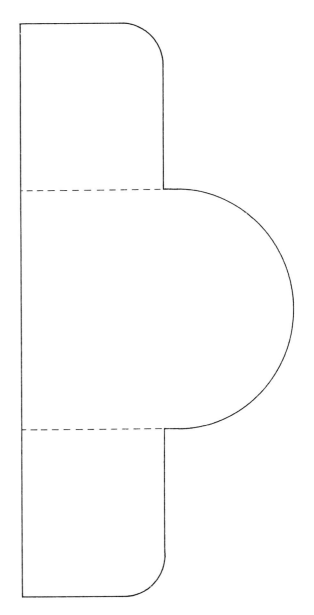

Fig 30 PATTERN FOR BEDROOM ARMCHAIR

SHOEBOX ROOMS

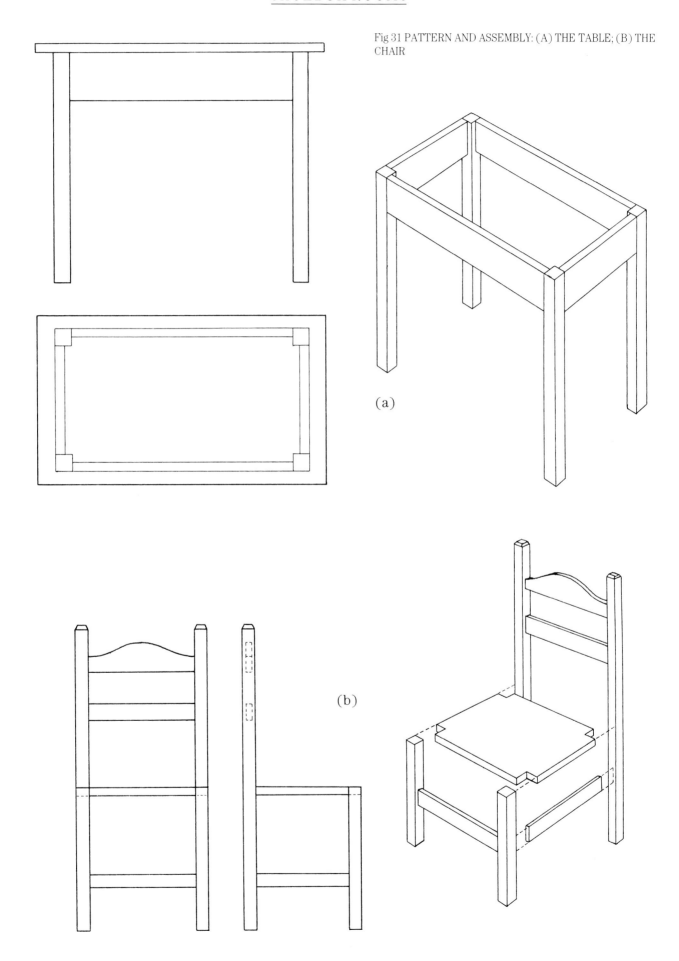

Fig 31 PATTERN AND ASSEMBLY: (A) THE TABLE; (B) THE CHAIR

(a)

(b)

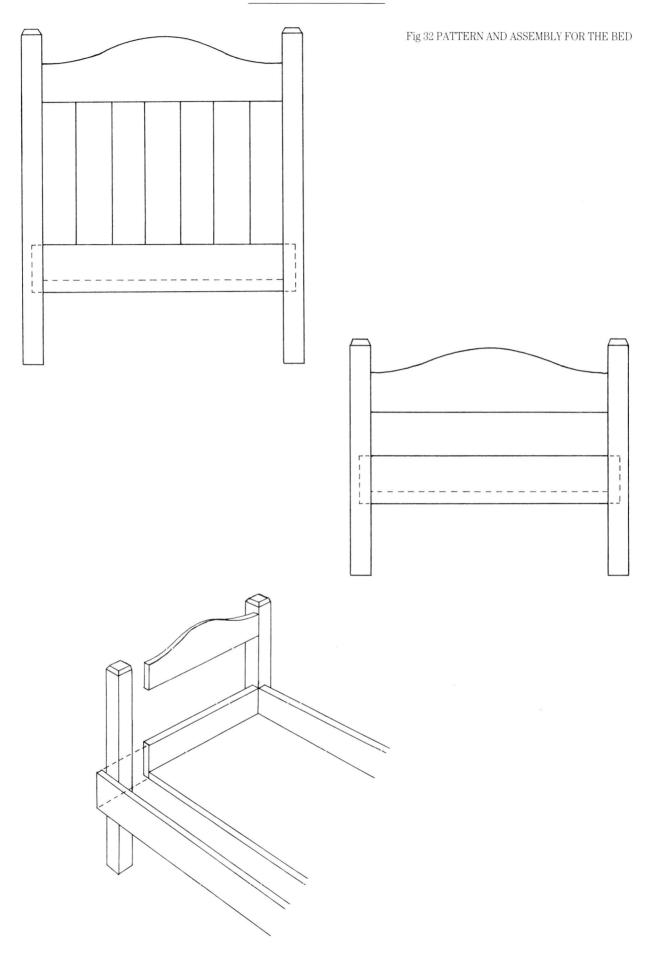

Fig 32 PATTERN AND ASSEMBLY FOR THE BED

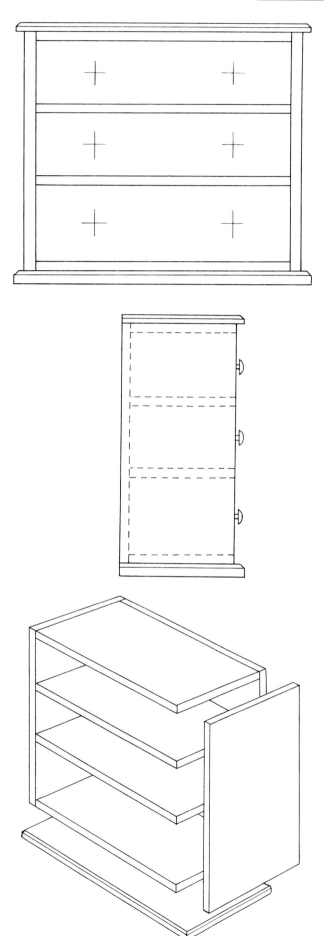

WARDROBE · To build the carcase of the wardrobe, cut two sides, one back, a top, bottom and drawer divider (see Fig 34). Glue the back to one side. Glue the top, bottom and drawer divider to the back and side. (Note that the bottom is cut from $\frac{1}{4}$in thick wood.) Drill a hole in both sides to receive the hanging rail. Cut the rail of $\frac{1}{16}$in diameter dowelling. Glue the second side in place, locating the dowelling rail in the drilled holes.

The doors are hinged with dressmaker's pins. Cut the doors to fit snugly into the front. Sand the hinged edges of the doors slightly rounded so that they will swing freely. Bore a fine hole with a dressmaker's pin into the top and bottom corners of the doors, as close as possible to the edge, taking care to work gently so that the wood does not split. Push pins into the holes and snip off to leave approximately $\frac{3}{32}$in protruding. Reverse the pins so that the pointed ends now protrude. Position the doors to mark the placement for the pin holes in the top and bottom of the carcase. Bore holes in the bottom to locate the pins. Bore holes through the top. Remove the pins from the top of the doors and locate the pins in the bottom of the doors into the holes that have been bored to receive them. Push the top pins through the top and into the top of the doors. Check that the doors swing freely, then push the pins fully into place.

Cut the pediment in wood $\frac{3}{8}$ x $\frac{1}{4}$in. This might be simply chamfered with a small plane, moulded using a shaper table, or you can use commercial moulding. Cut the pieces, mitring the corners, and glue in place.

The base is cut in $\frac{1}{8}$in wood, the edges are chamfered and the corners are mitred and glued in place.

The drawer is assembled by the instructions given in 'Making Furniture' in Chapter 1, using the simpler first method.

The wardrobe is finished by gluing a fine piece of thin wood-strip to the edge of one door, overlapping the other door. Escutcheon pins, glued into drilled holes, are used for door and drawer handles. Sand and paint the exterior of the wardrobe and the drawer front as required.

Fig 33 PATTERN AND ASSEMBLY FOR THE CHEST-OF-DRAWERS

Fig 34 PATTERN AND ASSEMBLY FOR THE WARDROBE

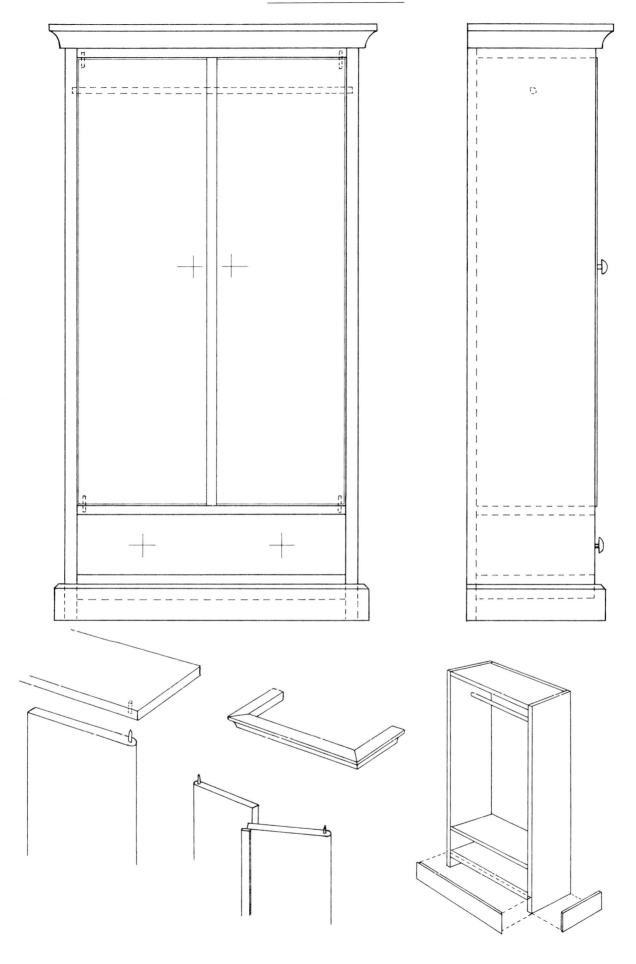

41

BEDDING · The bed has a ½in thick foam mattress, cut to fit the bed base and covered with cotton fabric, boxed at the corners. The small stuffed pillow has a pillowcase to match the sheets in fine cream cotton. The blanket is made of flannelette, blanket-stitched all the way around the edges, and the bedspread has a frill at the sides and bottom.

ACCESSORIES · The dolls' house is made from a free leaflet advertising home loans from the National Westminster Bank. The lamp and pictures are made the same way as those in the sitting-room.

The tennis racquet and ball are from Polly Flinders (see list of stockists, p177). The instructions for making the apple are given on p56 and the toffees are a magazine picture wrapped around a small block of wood.

The coloured pencils are cut from cocktail sticks, coloured with felt pens, in a 'glass' cut from an empty ink cartridge. The building bricks are small beads in a tub cut from a tube of tooth-cleaning tablets. The scrapbook is made of typing paper with tiny cut-out pictures glued in and the toys are all key-ring novelties from the local toyshop. The clock is a cut-out stuck to a button.

The carpet is Dralon velvet and the bedside rug is a small piece of white fur fabric, backed with iron-on Vilene.

RAG DOLLS

The shoebox dolls are very simple one-piece rag dolls, made in closely woven cotton fabric, eg calico.

The hair is made of embroidery silk (one skein per doll) and the features are drawn on with fine-point marker pens. Good quality polyester or terylene stuffing is recommended. The dolls may be dressed in scraps of any suitable fine cotton fabric, trimmed with scraps of narrow lace and ribbon. The dolls' shoes are made of felt. Patterns are given for child-size and adult-size dolls – the method is the same for both (Fig 35).

Draw the pattern onto a double thickness of fabric, squarely on the grain, and right side in. The drawn line is the sewing line. Stitch all the way around the drawn line with small firm stitches – do not leave a gap for turning through. Cut out the doll, approximately ¼in outside the stitched outline. With small sharp scissors, clip under the arms and the crotch and cut a slit in the back of the doll as shown on the pattern. Turn right side out through the slit, stuff the doll firmly and ladder stitch the slit closed. Stab stitch through the body at the shoulders and hips so that the limbs will bend. Use matching strong thread bound tightly around the limbs to define the elbows, wrists and knees. Bend the feet forward and ladder stitch the darts shown on the pattern to shape the feet and ankles.

Plate 4 THE SHOEBOX BEDROOM

3
MERMAIDS

This little fantasy inside a goldfish bowl can be made with any small 'fishy' items you choose. We have used an ordinary glass bowl from the local pet shop, a well-shaped rock from the beach and a selection of aquarium plants, lichen and small twigs for driftwood. The dried seahorse and the shells are from a beach shop at the nearest seaside resort and the glass fishing-floats are beads. The lobster and lobster-pot are from Carol Lodder (see list of stockists, p177). The mermaids are made from all-porcelain girl dolls from Dijon Importers, but if you prefer to model your own dolls, see pp128–31.

Buy a good-quality glass goldfish bowl so that the glass does not distort – check by putting your hand inside and looking at it from all angles. You will need about 1lb of clean sand and this may also be bought from a pet shop.

Before you begin, make a circular cardboard template of the area inside the bowl – measure across the bowl about 1½in above the bottom and cut a circle with this diameter. This will give you the area of your display and enable you to plan the pieces without having to keep taking things in and out of the bowl.

SAND BASE · To make a firm sandy base in the bottom of the bowl, use sand mixed with wallpaper paste. Make up about 1pt of wallpaper paste and stir the sand into it until the mixture is like a thick fruit-cake mixture. Spoon the sand/paste mix into the bowl and spread it out with the back of the spoon, checking that it is level. The mix will take some time to dry thoroughly, but you can speed the process by using a hair-dryer. Blow-dry the mixture in short blasts so that the glass does not overheat and crack. While the sand is drying, plan your display on the cardboard template.

Choose a flat-bottomed, attractively shaped and coloured rock which is large enough for the mermaid to sit on but small enough to leave room for other items. It is worth collecting an assortment of rocks, from the beach, from country lanes or from your garden, so that you can choose the one which looks best when you make the mermaids.

MERMAIDS · The Dijon dolls have porcelain heads and bodies in one piece, with arms and legs strung with knotted elastic. They are sold wigged and dressed. To make the mermaids, remove the wig and clothes and cut the elastic which holds the arms and legs. Keep the arms, which will be replaced later, and keep the wig if you do not wish to make a new one, but you will not need the legs. Traces of glue left on the doll's head will wipe away with a damp cloth.

The mermaid's tail is modelled in self-hardening clay, Das or a similar material available from art and craft shops. The one we recommend is 'La Doll' from Recollect Studios (see list of stockists, p176). Working with just the head and torso, the tail is modelled onto the body. Dampen the body slightly with water to achieve a good bond and shape a tail slightly longer than the head and torso. When the tail is a good shape, try the mermaid on the rock (covered with cling-film to prevent her from sticking to it) and arrange the tail in the position you want. Leave the doll on the rock until the tail has dried – with most air-drying clays this will be about forty-eight hours, but you can use the hair-dryer to speed things up. The second mermaid is made in the same way, with her tail curved gracefully to sit on the sand. When the tail is thoroughly dry, gently sand it with fine abrasive paper until it is completely smooth.

The tails are painted with Humbrol enamel paints in metallic colours. We have used gold and green for one mermaid and silver and blue for the other. Paint the tail with one coat of the basic colour (gold or silver) and allow it to dry thoroughly. Paint a second coat of the basic colour and, while this is still wet, streak in touches of the second colour. The two colours will blend together as they dry. The glittering effect is made by painting on glitter suspended in glue. This type of glitter, called Guterman-Dekor, is available in tubes from some haberdashery departments and comes in a range of colours. Both mermaids illustrated here have been painted with No 668, a mixture of blue and green glitter. The mixture is squeezed onto the tail and brushed out all over. As it dries, the white glue disappears completely, leaving the glittering effect of scales.

When the tails are completed, reattach the doll's arms. This may be done by knotting a length of hat elastic, passing it through the hole in one arm, through the body and through the hole in the other arm, stretching it taut and knotting the other end. A neater method is to use a piece of fine dowelling through the body and pushed into the holes in each arm, filled with modelling clay. When the clay is dry, the arms are held securely, without the knots of elastic which inevitably show if you use the other method.

If you are retaining the doll's original wig, replace it with a little UHU glue applied to the head. We made new wigs in greeny-blonde mohair (from Sunday Dolls – see list of stockists p177). Smooth out a length of mohair and stitch a parting through the centre with tiny back stitches. Style the wig in your fingers so that the hair falls to the back and sides, then coat the doll's head with UHU glue and carefully position the wig. One doll wears a wreath of tiny pearls, the other a wisp of aquarium weed.

ACCESSORIES · Arrange the pieces on the cardboard template. Position the rock, glue the mermaid in position (with UHU) and glue a half shell filled with tiny pearls onto her lap. Strands of 'seaweed' are glued to the rock and the dried seahorse is glued in place. If you find a similar dried seahorse will not take the position you want, soak it in warm water to make it pliable – seahorses are fragile, though, so handle them gently. If you prefer, the seahorse may be painted with two or three coats of gold paint and the eyes touched in with black. Arrange the second mermaid, the lobster and pot, shells, fishing floats and driftwood to make a pleasing all-round picture. Where an object touches the rock, glue it in place so that as much of the display as possible can be put into the bowl in one go. The fishing-net draped over the lobster-pot is made from a piece of the bright red net which holds fruit bought from the supermarket. It was soaked in dark brown poster paint and dried thoroughly, then glued around the pot. The lobster is glued to the mermaid's lap.

When the sand in the bowl is thoroughly dry, clean the inside of the bowl with window cleaner and kitchen paper, then squeeze a 'puddle' of UHU glue onto the sand where the rock will be placed. Let the glue become tacky, then carefully place the rock, with the mermaid sitting on it and the pieces which are stuck to it. Squeeze a small puddle of glue onto the sand and, when it is tacky, position the second mermaid. Check the display from all angles and decide where there are bare areas which need to be filled. Weed, twigs, groups of shells, etc can then be glued and positioned in these areas. A long pair of tweezers makes the job easier. When the display is complete, clean and polish the outside of the goldfish bowl.

Plate 5 MERMAIDS

Plate 6 MERMAIDS

MARKET STALLS

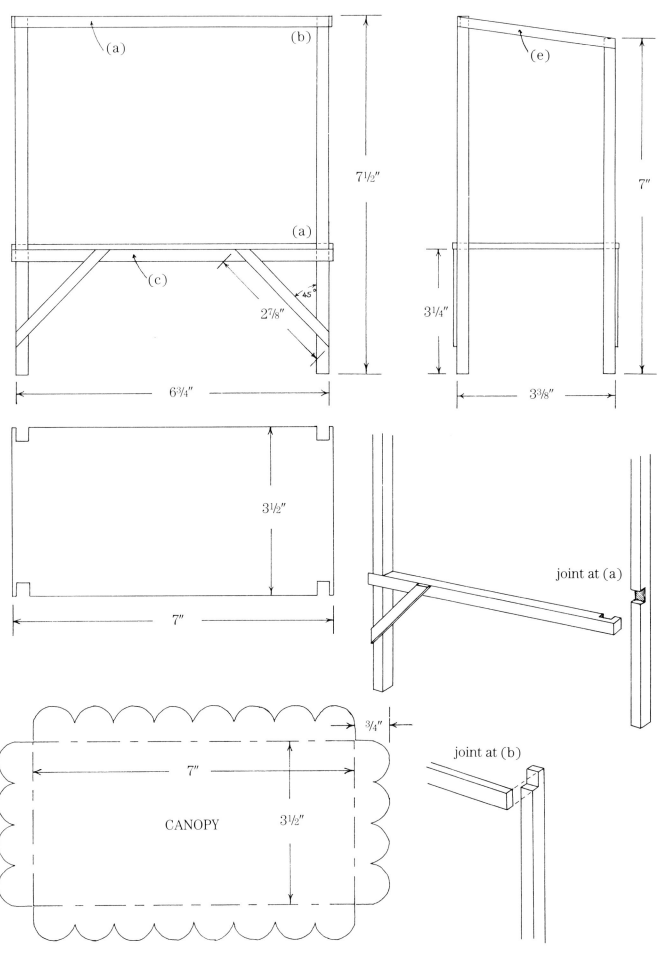

(a)

(b)

(e)

7½"

(a)

(c)

45°

2⅞"

6¾"

7"

3¼"

3⅜"

3½"

7"

joint at (a)

¾"

7"

CANOPY

3½"

joint at (b)

Fig 37 THE MARKET STALL

48

4
MARKET STALLS

Market stalls are a splendid way to display a collection of small bought or made miniatures. The stock might be anything which takes your fancy – pottery, bread and cakes, or haberdashery. Here is a place for hats if you don't want to open a shop, or a place for toys if you do not have a nursery.

The stall and the barrow are simple to make and can be decorated in any way you please. Both stand on wooden bases – one represents grass and the other cobbles. 'Russel Sprout' is a modelled doll from Thames Valley Craft, but if you prefer to model your own, see Chapter 9, pp128–31.

ANTIQUE STALL

To make the stall, you will need approximately 5ft of ¼in square hardwood. The counter is made from a piece of ⅛in thick plywood. The wood is available from DIY shops. you will also need a 3ft length of ¼in wood-strip (available from model shops).

To make the construction simple and sturdy, all the joints are cross-halved (see Fig 37). Where one length of wood crosses another, notches are cut in each piece to a depth of ⅛in so that when the pieces are glued together, they interlock. Cut the notches by marking the position with a sharp pencil, then use a fine-toothed razor saw to cut to a depth of ⅛in. Use a craft knife or small chisel to cut out the joint. Assemble the pieces with white woodwork glue.

Cut two pairs of upright posts. (The back posts are ½in shorter than the front posts.) Cut two counter supports (c) in ¼in wood and two canopy (d) supports in wood-strip. Assemble the front and back posts separately. Joint the front posts to one counter support and canopy support; glue the joints and allow to dry. Assemble the back posts and supports in the same way.

Cut the counter and notch the four corners as shown on the pattern. (Note that these notches are cut 3/16in deep.) Glue the front post assembly into the counter, ensuring a perfect right angle. Glue the back post assembly into the counter, also ensuring the right angle.

Cut the wood-strip pieces (e) to fit across the top of the front and back posts and glue in place.

Cut four struts in wood-strip to fit diagonally across the posts and the counter supports. Glue the struts in place.

Sand and paint the stall as required. We used Humbrol enamel paint, a matt undercoat and two gloss top coats, sanded between each coat.

CANOPY · The canopy (see Fig 37) is made from a scrap of cotton drill. Draw the outline onto the fabric and paint Fraycheck or glue around the drawn line. When this is dry, cut it out. Fold and press along the dotted lines shown on the pattern so that the sides of the canopy will hang well.

The stall is covered with a cotton cloth – the edges turned under and glued in place.

BACK SUPPORT

BOTTOM SHELF

SIDE (CUT 2)

Fig 38 PATTERN FOR DISPLAY SHELVES FOR MARKET STALL

TOP SHELF

Plate 7 MARKET STALL

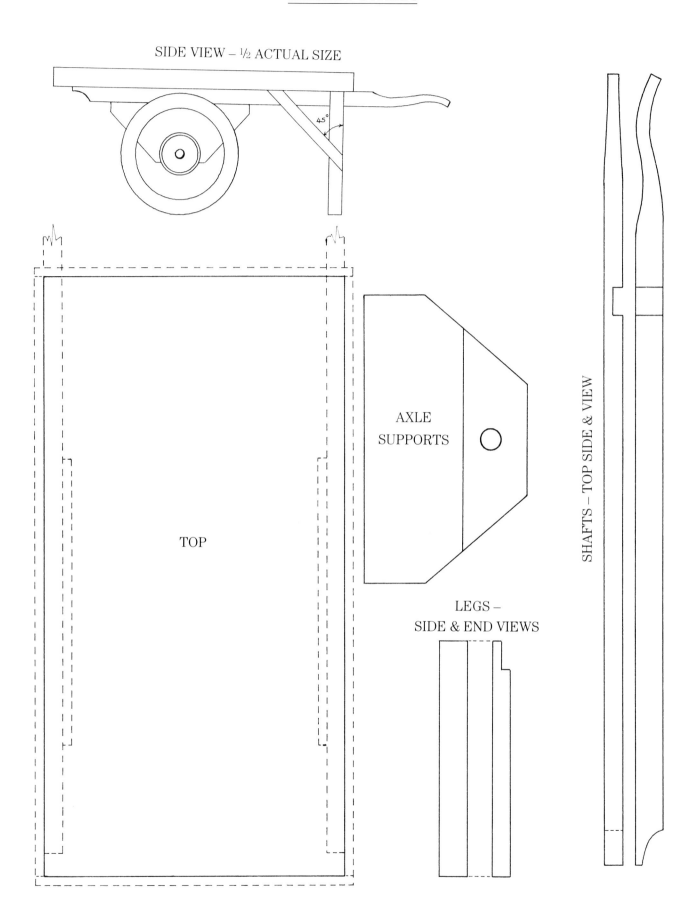

SIDE VIEW – ½ ACTUAL SIZE

45°

TOP

AXLE
SUPPORTS

LEGS –
SIDE & END VIEWS

SHAFTS – TOP SIDE & VIEW

Fig 39 PATTERN FOR THE BARROW

SHELVES · To make the display shelves, use ³⁄₃₂in thick wood. Cut two sides, both shelves and the back support from the pattern (Fig 38). To hold things steady while you work, wedge both side pieces into a little Blu-tack on the work surface. Glue the two shelves in place across the sides. When this is dry, glue the support across the back. Paint as required.

STOCK · The stall has been filled with a collection of miniature bric-a-brac items including china Sussex dogs, a 'Sèvres' clock and a 'Rockingham' castle from Recollect Studios (see list of stockists, p176).

BASE · The stall stands on a base board made of ³⁄₈in plywood. Cut a piece of plywood 9 x 6in and sand the top and bottom and all edges thoroughly smooth. Cover the top of the board with a piece of grass-effect paper (available from craft and model shops) cut to fit and glued in place with UHU. The edges of the board are faced with ³⁄₈in wide, ¹⁄₈in thick wood-strip, stained with walnut wood stain and glued in place with contact adhesive; the corners are mitred. The underside of the base board may be covered with felt or flocked Fablon if required. The legs of the stall can be glued to the base with UHU, used sparingly.

RUSSEL SPROUT – QUALITY FRUIT AND VEG

BARROW · To make the barrow you will need a piece of ¹⁄₈in thick plywood 3¹⁄₄ x 6¹⁄₄in, a length of ³⁄₃₂in thick obeche wood, a 2ft length of ¹⁄₄in hardboard, ¹⁄₂in wide (from DIY shops), a 6in length of ³⁄₁₆in dowelling and a pair of 2¹⁄₂in diameter wheels. We have used Hobby's plastic cartwheels which are available directly from Hobby's (see Magazines, p175) or from most model shops.

Cut ¹⁄₂in wide strips of obeche wood and glue them around the plywood to make the barrow top (see Fig 39).

Plane the hardwood to the dimensions shown on the pattern for the shafts and carve the handles with a craft knife.

Cut two legs and cross halve (see the stall) these into the shafts. Glue the shafts to the underside of the barrow top as shown in Fig 39. To make the axle supports, cut the two pieces as shown on the pattern for each support in ³⁄₃₂in obeche wood and glue the smaller pieces to the larger ones. Drill holes as shown through the supports to fit the dowelling axle. This hole should fit the hole in the hubs of the wheels you are using. Glue the axle supports to the underside of the barrow top as shown and allow to dry thoroughly (Fig 40).

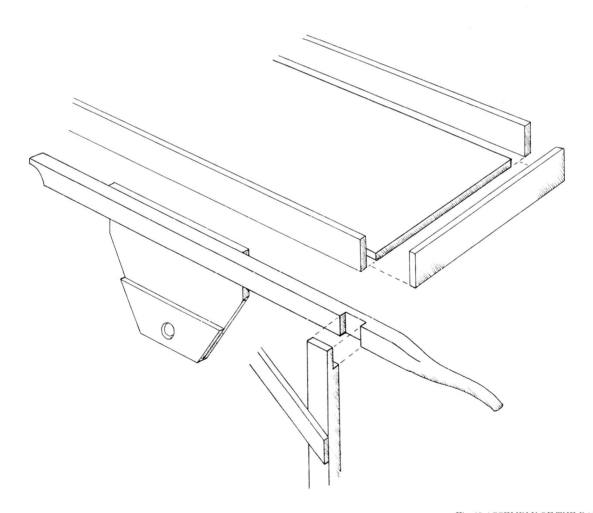

Fig 40 ASSEMBLY OF THE BARROW

Plate 8 RUSSEL SPROUT:
QUALITY FRUIT AND VEG

Fit the axle through the holes in the axle supports and fit the wheels. Drill a small hole through the axle on the outside of one wheel to take an axle pin made from a bent paper-clip. Trim the axle on the outer side of the other wheel and drill the hole for the axle pin, but do not fit the second axle pin until the model is painted. Remove the wheels and axle for painting. The barrow was painted with Humbrol enamel gloss paint, green for the barrow and red and yellow for the wheels. The wheel rims and the axle are painted with matt black enamel paint. The sign on the end of the barrow is made with Letraset on cream cardboard and framed with thin wood-strip painted red.

BASE · The barrow stands on a base board made of ³⁄₈in thick plywood, measuring 10 x 6in. The board is covered with 'cobblestones' made in self-hardening clay. Roll out the clay (eg Das), on a flat board with an old rolling-pin, until you have a piece about 12 x 8in and about ⅛in thick. Use a tool with a blunt point, eg a stylus or small knitting-needle, to mark out rows of cobbles. The cobbles are approximately ¼in wide and ½in long. It takes time and patience, but each cobble should be shaped, rounding the edges and corners and flattening the surface. Aim for a fairly regular, but not too regular, effect. Allow the cobbles to dry thoroughly, turning the sheet over from time to time as it curls up at the edges. The drying out will take about two days, but can be speeded up with a hair-dryer. If the sheet seems to be curling up too much, press it under a heavy weight, but this clay is fairly pliable and can usually be pressed flat again with the hand. When the sheet is thoroughly dry, cut the area you need to fit the base board (all in one piece) and glue it in place by smearing UHU all over the board and pressing the sheet of clay firmly in place. Use the craft knife to round off the sharp corners around the outside edge, then sand the cobbles gently with fine-grade abrasive paper and remove all traces of dust.

Use poster or acrylic paints to paint the cobbles. Mix shades of dark grey, dark brown, dark green and mid-grey on a plate, using the paint quite thick. Paint these colours, and mixtures of these colours, onto the cobbles, picking out individual stones in different colours – cobbles are not all grey. Make sure that you work the paint thoroughly into all the cracks and around the outside edges. The paint will dry a lighter colour and you may need a second coat if you have not used it thickly enough or have misjudged the colours. When the paint is thoroughly dry, the base board is edged with ³⁄₈in wide thin wood-strip which has been stained with walnut wood-stain and glued to the edges with contact adhesive; the corners should be mitred. The cobbles stand proud above the top edge of the wood-strip. The barrow may be stuck to the cobbles with a little UHU glue under the wheels and the shafts, but if you later remove it, it will take the paint off the stones and they will have to be retouched.

BOXES · To make the boxes for the fruit and vegetables, use ¹⁄₁₆in obeche wood for the bases and ¹⁄₁₆in wood-strip for the sides. Sand or plane the wood-strip to ¹⁄₃₂in to give the boxes more realistic proportions. Cut the sides and base for each box and assemble them with the base inside the sides. To make the triangular struts in each corner, chamfer along the edge of a sheet of ⅛in thick obeche wood to make a 45° angle. Using a fine-toothed razor saw, cut the triangular section. Cut the required lengths and glue them into the corners of each box. Glue a length of the finest wood-strip across both sides to form handles. Mark the staples on the boxes with pencil. If you want an aged effect, paint a wash of greeny-black paint over the boxes. Use tiny labels peeled from oranges, or print shippers' labels onto the boxes with fine-tipped felt pens.

FRUIT AND VEGETABLES · The fruit and vegetables are best made in Fimo (available from art and craft shops). Fimo is easy to work with, has a good texture and comes in a wide range of colours which can be mixed to make the exact colours of any fruit or vegetable. Fimo makes the job easier as the produce has only to be modelled and not painted – colour-matching and painting these tiny items is very tricky. If you invest in the full set of thirty Fimo colours, you will have little mixing to do and colours to model almost any item you want, but for Russel Sprout's stock you can manage with just light and dark green, orange, yellow, red, beige, brown, white and transparent. Modelled items are baked in a domestic oven at 265°F (130°C) to harden and this will take about 10 minutes. Cover a baking sheet with greaseproof paper and model all the items before you bake them. This can be done over a period of time as Fimo will not dry out or harden until it is baked; this is more economical than cooking a few pieces at a time. It is very helpful to have the life-size item in front of you when making the miniature, as a guide for colour, shape and size. If you match the colour exactly, the imagination will make up for any deficiencies in the modelling – but do make things tiny. If you have a doll, use it as a guide on size.

Oranges Roll tiny balls of orange Fimo and press the pointed end of a wooden toothpick gently into the top to indent it. When baked, paint a brown dot into this indent.

Apples Roll light green balls – smaller than for oranges – indent the tops and push in a tiny piece of dried pine-needle for a stalk. Green will do for Golden Delicious, but for a Cox's apple, dab on a little rusty-red paint when it is baked.

Peaches Roll red and yellow Fimo together to obtain a marbled effect. Roll into balls and use a wooden toothpick to mark the crease. Dust lightly with talcum powder to make the 'bloom'.

Bananas Mix yellow with a little white. Roll sausage shapes tapered at both ends and make bunches of four to six. When baked, paint areas of pale green on some bananas (not quite ripe) and with a very fine brush, mark brown spots and streaks on others. Paint the stalk end of each bunch brown.

Grapefruit Mix yellow and white Fimo and roll into balls. Indent one end and, when baked, paint a tiny brown spot in the indented end.

Grapes Mix light green and transparent Fimo and roll into very tiny balls. Use a small twig to represent the stalk and gently press a small handful of grapes together around the twig.

Potatoes Roll beige Fimo into irregular rounded shapes. When baked, roll them in real potato dust.

Carrots Roll orange Fimo into tiny sausage shapes, then taper one end and flatten the other. When baked, use a very fine brush to mark lines around the carrots and circles at the flattened ends with brown paint.

Onions Mix brown and transparent Fimo and roll into small balls. Roll one side of the ball between the fingers so that it forms a tapering point. When baked, paint on brown patches and streaks and use tiny pieces of real onion skin for display.

Cauliflower Mix white and transparent Fimo and roll a ball for the heart. Use a toothpick to make a crunkled effect on the heart. Use dark green for the leaves, pinched as thinly as possible between the fingers and torn into shape. Build up three or four leaves around the heart.

Cabbage or lettuce Mix light green and transparent Fimo. Pinch as thinly as possible between the fingers and tear leaf shapes. Build up the leaves, keeping the base fairly flat.

Tomatoes Roll red Fimo into small balls and indent one end of each. When baked, paint green star shapes into the indents with a fine brush.

Sweetcorn Use yellow Fimo for the cob, rolled to a sausage shape, and tapered at both ends. Press light green Fimo flat between the fingers and tear the leaves to shape. Wrap two or three leaves around the cob.

Peppers Make balls of red or green Fimo. Squeeze gently between the fingers to shape the sides and indent both ends. When baked, paint green stalks into the indent at one end.

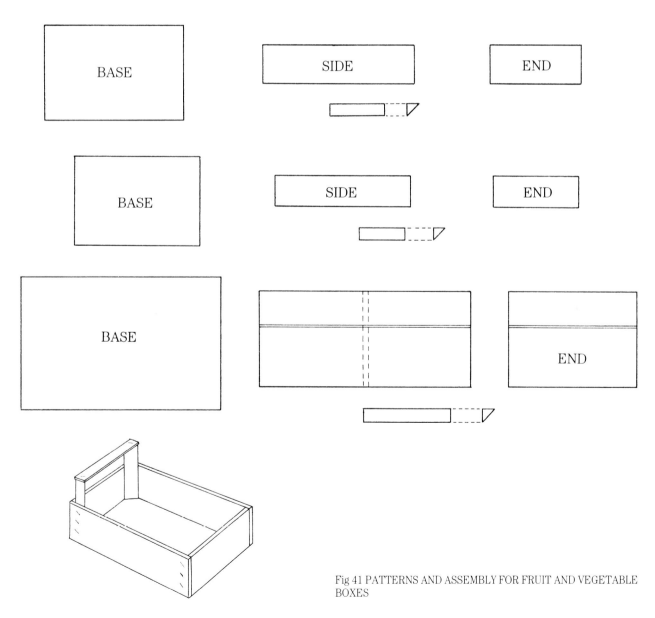

Fig 41 PATTERNS AND ASSEMBLY FOR FRUIT AND VEGETABLE BOXES

Plate 9 RUSSEL SPROUT: FRUIT AND VEGETABLE BARROW

Many other fruit and vegetables might be made, but space on Russel's stall is limited and we have used those he would most likely sell. If you don't wish to model the produce, splendid fruit and vegetables can be bought from Wentways Miniatures (see list of stockists, p177) who make all those described here and many more.

ACCESSORIES · The boxes are lined and some of the fruit wrapped in blue tissue-paper. To get exactly the right sort it is best to scrounge a couple of used pieces from your local greengrocer. We have used two shades, a dark blue and a paler, almost lilac colour. The price tickets are made of postcard. Small rectangles are drawn on the card with red felt pen, then the prices are marked with a fine (Rotring) drawing-pen. The cards are cut out and taped to dressmaker's pins which are pushed into the produce or boxes. The brown paper-bags (Fig 42) made from a life-size grocery bag, are folded, glued together with UHU and strung by button thread from a small brass pin in the barrow handle.

The metal scales, painted red and green are from The Mulberry Bush and the basket of potatoes is from Thames Valley Crafts (see list of stockists, p176).

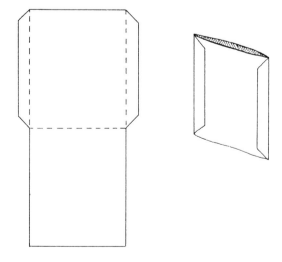

Fig 42 PATTERN FOR PAPER-BAGS

5
VIGNETTES

The word 'vignette' in the miniatures' world is used to describe a small scene inside a picture frame. The scene is necessarily shallow – usually no more than 6in – so the vignette gives the effect of a three-dimensional picture. Despite its limited depth, the vignette offers a great deal of scope as the 'picture' may be as large or as small as you please. It might be only 6in wide and used to display just one piece of furniture or a beautiful doll, or as large as 24in wide and furnished as an elaborate drawing-room. The choice of subject is only limited by your imagination.

Our two vignettes represent 'The night before Christmas' and 'The dollmaker's workroom'. They are both 10 x 8in and are designed to fit standard-size commercial picture frames, available from art shops or picture-framers. The vignette is made in plywood, as a simple box, and the picture frame is hinged onto the front to allow access. Both boxes are made in the same way.

TO MAKE THE VIGNETTE BOX · Cut the pieces shown on the pattern (Fig 43, p60) in ¼in thick plywood for the sides and ⅛in plywood for the back. Assemble the pieces with white woodwork glue and ⅝in veneer pins. Glue and pin the sides to either side of the top and bottom, and glue and pin the back in place. Sand the box thoroughly and finish the outside. Three coats of satin finish emulsion paint, sanded between each coat, have been used.

The frame, chosen to complement the scene inside the box, is hinged with two 1in brass hinges so that it opens like a door. Screw the hinges to the outside of the box, flush with the front edge (see Fig 43). Fit the frame in place and mark the hinges on the back of the frame. Screw the other half of the hinge flat to the frame. The frame is glazed with perspex which is lighter than glass and can be held in place with a little UHU glue.

To support the box behind the frame, small feet, made of dowelling or purchased from DIY shops, are glued to the underside of the box.

We recommend that the box is decorated outside and inside before the frame is hinged in place. If necessary, a small cupboard hook can be fitted to hold the front closed.

THE NIGHT BEFORE CHRISTMAS

CHIMNEY-BREAST · The chimney-breast is built of 1in thick balsa wood, faced with ⅛in thick obeche wood (or plywood). The dimensions are shown in Fig 44. Cut both balsa and obeche wood to these dimensions and glue the obeche piece to the front of the balsa with wood glue. Clamp the two pieces together and allow the glue to dry. Facing the balsa in this way builds up the full depth required to accommodate the fireplace and provides a good surface for decorating.

A white metal kit from Phoenix Model Developments has been used to make the tiled 'Coalbrookdale' fireplace and fender, and the dimensions given on the pattern for the fireplace opening are designed to fit this fireplace. If you are using a different fireplace, the size of the opening should be adjusted accordingly.

Sand the chimney-breast thoroughly and glue it to the wall with wood glue.

CORNICE · We have used dolls' house cornice and picture-rail mouldings from Hobby's (see Magazines, p175). You will need 24in of both for this project. The mouldings will need a thorough sanding with fine abrasive paper to make them completely smooth before use. Install the cornice, unpainted, but the picture-rail should be painted before it is fitted.

Cut a cardboard template of the appropriate depth and use this to mark the position of the picture-rail all the way around the walls to ensure a perfectly straight line.

Starting with the back wall in each alcove and working forward, cut pieces of cornice and picture-rail to fit each wall, mitring the corners, and glue them in place. If necessary, fill any cracks or gaps between the cornice and the ceiling or walls with a little Polyfilla (or similar) applied with a kitchen knife and rubbed in with a damp finger.

FIREPLACE · Chapter 8 includes a discussion on white metal kits (see pp112–13) and you may find it useful to read this before assembling a similar fireplace.

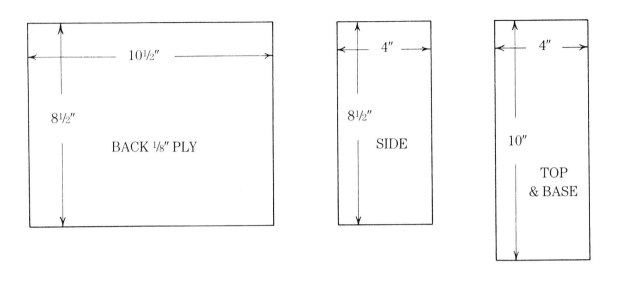

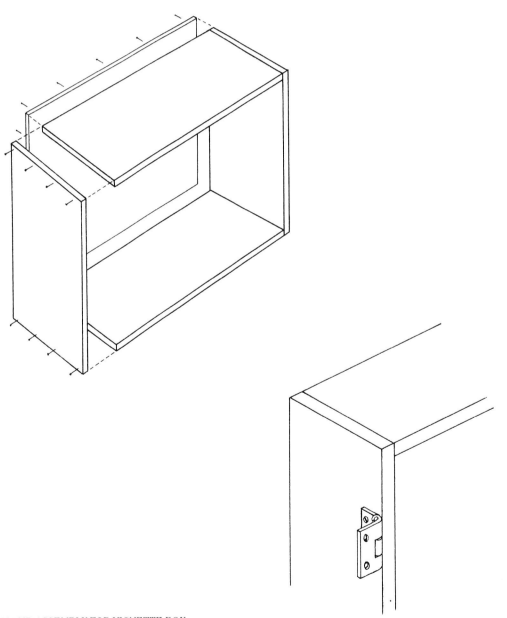

Fig 43 PATTERN AND ASSEMBLY FOR VIGNETTE BOX

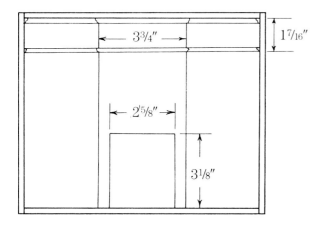

CHIMNEY BREAST 1⅛" deep

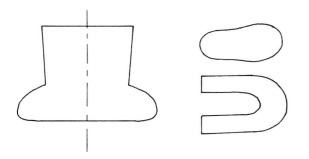

Fig 44 FIREPLACE DIMENSIONS AND STOCKING AND SLIPPER PATTERNS

Clean the fireplace and assemble with epoxy resin adhesive. The fireplace is painted before it is glued in place. Prime the piece with matt white Humbrol enamel paint. We have painted the surround to represent wood using brown gloss enamel paint. The centre arch is painted matt dark grey and the details in a lighter grey. The tiles are painted with thinned paint, one coat of the background colour (matt cream) and the pattern in gloss paint, blue and red, using a very fine brush. The fender is primed and painted with two coats of Humbrol metallic brass paint.

Paint the inside of the fireplace opening with matt black paint, before decorating the room.

DECORATING · The walls above the picture-rail, the cornice and the ceiling are painted with two coats of magnolia matt emulsion paint. The picture-rail is painted with Humbrol enamel paint in ivory gloss. Paint a length of ⅜in wide thin wood-strip with ivory gloss for the skirting-board, but do not glue it in place until the walls are papered. We have used a commercial dolls' house wallpaper, but you may prefer a small-patterned wrapping paper or life-size wallpaper. Size the walls with a coat of wallpaper paste and, when this is dry, paste and hang the wallpaper. When the wallpaper is dry, cut the skirting-boards to fit with mitred corners in the alcoves and around the chimney-breast and glue in place with UHU. Glue the assembled fireplace in position (with

UHU) after the walls are papered and fit the front pieces of skirting-board on either side. The floor was papered with a wood-effect dolls' house floor paper stuck with wallpaper paste, and a small hearth of paper tiles, cut from a magazine illustration, was glued inside the fireplace.

FIRE · The fire is made from red and gold tinsel braid, small pieces of coal, glue and cigarette ash. Crumple a 6in length of tinsel braid and glue it into the grate. Squeeze a 'puddle' of glue (the type of glue which disappears as it dries, such as Aileens tacky-glue from Sunday Dolls – see list of stockists, p177) onto the braid and drop a small handful of tiny pieces of coal onto the glue. Squeeze a puddle of glue onto the coal and drop cigarette ash onto the glue. The 'smoke' is a wisp of polyester stuffing, teased out and placed over the fire. This method makes a very effective fire, as both the coal and the ash are real.

The mantelshelf over the fireplace was made from ⅜in thick obeche wood, ½in wide, mounted on small brackets of picture-frame moulding. The mantelshelf is painted to match the fireplace surround and glued to the wall with UHU glue.

The rug is a woven Turkish rug from Mini Marvels (see list of stockists, p176) which is 4in wide. It was cut to fit around the chimney-breast and the cut edges were sealed with Fraycheck (or glue) to prevent them from unravelling.

FURNITURE · The armchair is made from a kit from Jennifer's of Walsall (see list of stockists, p176). Chapter 7, pp86–7 includes full notes on making up furniture kits and you may find it helpful to read this before making a similar chair. We covered the chair in crimson velveteen rather than the fabric supplied because it suited the room decor. The little wine table is also made from a kit and both pieces were stained with mahogany wood stain and wax polished.

TREE · The Christmas tree is made from dowelling and green chenille stems, available from art and craft shops, and stands in a brown plastic bottle-cap pot. To make the tree, cut a length of fine dowelling (or a paint-brush handle) the height of the finished tree – the one illustrated is 5½in tall. Mix a little plaster of Paris or Polyfilla and fix the dowelling into the centre of the pot. When the plaster is dry, paint the top dark brown with poster or acrylic paint to represent earth. Fix the pot to the work surface with a little Blu-tack to hold it steady while you build the tree. Begin at the bottom and work upwards. Cut short lengths of chenille and twist these around slightly longer lengths, which are then twisted around the main 'branches' of the tree. The branches are twisted and glued around the dowelling in the centre. As you work upwards, each branch is shorter, but you must decide for yourself how many branches you want. Ensure that the tree is bushy enough to completely cover the dowelling but not so bushy that it looks clumsy.

Plate 10 THE NIGHT BEFORE
CHRISTMAS: VIGNETTE

The tree decorations are made of gold and silver beads and metallic sequins. To make a bauble, thread doubled fine fuse-wire through the bead and form a loop at the top to hang it by. Bend up the lower ends of the wire and glue to prevent the bead from slipping off. Baubles might have tiny beads at the top and bottom or be painted with enamel or acrylic paints and a fine brush. Sequins are wired in pairs to show different colours on each side, the wire passing through the holes in the sequins and twisted to make a loop at the top. The star at the top of the tree is made from star-shaped sequins with a tiny diamanté stone glued to the centre. The tinsel is sold in stationer's shops for tying Christmas parcels. Drape the tinsel around the tree and hang the baubles, pushing the chenille stems through the wire loops.

DECORATIONS · The holly wreath is made by twisting a length of green chenille stem into a circle and glueing on small sprays of holly. We used holly from Wentways Miniatures (see list of stockists, p177) but you might also consider the holly sprays sold for cake decoration. Trim the wreath with a bow of red ribbon and two tiny gold beads.

The paper chains are made from fine silk ribbons, two lengths placed together and glued to the picture-rail above the fireplace. Hold the two ribbons together and twist them until the twist reaches the front of the side walls, then trim and glue the ends to the picture-rail.

The Christmas cards are cut from magazine illustrations – in this case the Laura Ashley catalogue – but similar tiny pictures could be cut from parts of life-size cards. Paint out unwanted writing, etc with correcting fluid and write your own tiny good wishes inside the cards.

ACCESSORIES · The presents under the tree are made from small scraps of wood and other oddments covered in lightweight paper with small patterns. This is fiddly but is easier to do if the 'present' is glued to the paper first. Wrap and glue the paper as you go, using your thumb-nail to score sharp creases. Trim the parcels with fine ribbon and bows or tinsel. The presents look most effective if they are all different shapes and sizes and are wrapped in several different papers.

The stocking is made in red felt. Cut the pattern (Fig 44) and fold the piece in half. With tiny stitches, whip the edges together, down the leg, around the toe and under the foot. Turn through and trim the top edge with a scrap of fine white braid, glued in place. Glue the stocking to the edge of the mantelshelf.

The slippers under the chair may be made in any lightweight fabric which does not fray, eg felt. Cut one upper and one sole in fabric for each slipper and cut a pair of soles in postcard (Fig 44). Using tiny blanket stitches, sew the back seam on each upper on the wrong side, then sew the uppers to the soles on the right side. Slip the card soles inside the slippers.

We completed the picture with a pair of framed needle-point silhouettes from Linda Gibson, a box of chocolates from Jennifer's of Walsall, a china dog ornament from Recollect and a wine glass from Leo Pilley; the gilt-framed mirror is from The Mulberry Bush (see list of stockists pp176–7). The mince pies are modelled in Fimo, on a button plate decorated with a sprig of holly, and a small stuffed cushion is tucked into the corner of the armchair.

We chose an elaborate gilt frame to enhance the Christmas card effect, glazed with perspex and hinged on as described.

THE DOLLMAKER'S WORKROOM

DECORATING · The cornice, from Hobby's, is cut with mitred corners to fit the back and side walls and glued in place. Fill any gaps with Polyfilla (or similar). The cornice and ceiling are painted with two coats of magnolia emulsion paint and the walls are papered with a dolls' house wallpaper. The skirting-board (3/8in wide thin wood-strip) is painted with ivory Humbrol enamel gloss and glued in place after the carpet is fitted. The carpet is rust-coloured needlecord, cut with the selvage-edge to the front and glued to the floor around the edges with UHU. The skirting-board is cut to fit to each side of the corner unit.

FURNITURE · The furniture in this project is designed for more experienced miniaturists. Pine was used for the shelves and chest-of-drawers and cherry for the wall-shelf and table. The chair is made of yew and cherry. The construction methods are described in Chapter 1 pp12–26; you will need the basic tools, and a lathe to turn the chair and table legs. A shaper table, while not essential, will make cutting the grooves and joints simpler and quicker.

CORNER UNIT · Cut two sides from the pattern (note that one side is fractionally wider than the other – Fig 45) chamfering the front edges to an angle of 45°. Mark the position of the top, bottom and four shelves on both pieces. Use a craft knife, metal ruler and watchmaker's 'chisel' or the shaper table, to cut grooves on these marks to receive the shelves, top and bottom. Cut a rabbet down the back edge of the wider side piece.

Cut six triangular pieces from the pattern to make the shelves, top and bottom.

Glue the sides together, fitting one piece into the rabbet on the other. At the same time, glue the top and bottom into their grooves. This will ensure that the unit is held square. When these pieces are dry, glue the shelves into their grooves.

Cut the fascia pieces shown on the pattern and glue these in place to the front of the unit. Note that the top curved piece extends 1/8in above the unit.

The piece was stained with very dilute light oak stain, which gives the appearance of old pine, and finished with one coat of French polish, sanded and waxed on the front of the unit.

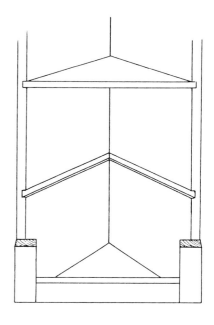

FIG 45 PATTERN AND ASSEMBLY FOR
THE CORNER UNIT

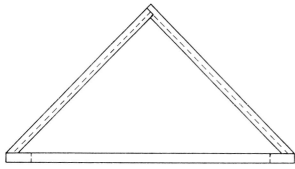

WALL-SHELF · Cut two sides with a fret-saw. Cut one shelf and one back rail. Use a needle file and fine sandpaper to smooth the curves. Mark and cut recesses to receive the shelf and back rail. Glue the sides to the shelf, ensuring that they are perfectly upright. Glue the back rail in place. The piece was finished with a very light coat of walnut stain and one coat of French polish, sanded and waxed.

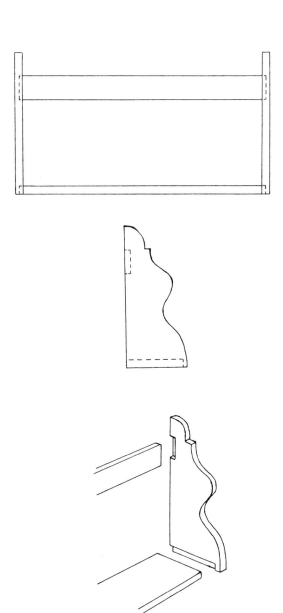

Fig 46 PATTERN AND ASSEMBLY FOR THE WALL-SHELF

Plate 11 THE DOLLMAKER'S WORKROOM: VIGNETTE

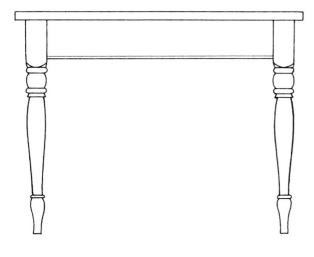

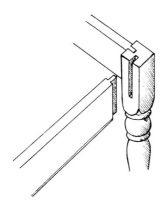

Fig 47 PATTERN AND ASSEMBLY FOR THE TABLE

TABLE · To turn the table legs, prepare four 3½in lengths of square-section wood to the dimension shown on the pattern (Fig 47). Chuck one length into the lathe and turn to the pattern. Ensure that you leave sufficient square-section wood at the bottom of the leg to support the piece if you are cutting joints on a shaper table. Refer to p24 in Chapter 1 for instructions on turning. Use the shaper table to cut joints on two sides of each leg, as shown in Fig 47. When these joints are cut, trim the excess wood from the ends of the legs, using dividers to ensure that the legs are of equal length.

Cut two pairs of friezes from the pattern – remember that the pieces must be cut long enough to make the joints. Chamfer the bottom outside edge of each frieze piece. Use the shaper table or craft knife to cut tenons at each end of the pieces. Assemble and glue a leg to each end of the long friezes. When these assemblies are thoroughly dry, glue the short friezes into the legs. Make this assembly upside-down on a perfectly flat work surface to ensure that the top of the assembly is completely level.

Cut the table-top, glue the top edge of the leg assembly and position the table-top, clamping it in place as the glue dries. The table was finished with a light coat of walnut stain and one coat of French polish, sanded and waxed.

CHAIR · The chair seat is made of cherry wood and all the other parts of yew (Fig 48). Cut the seat using a fret-saw – the grain should run from front to back. Mark a pencil line on the underside of the seat; perfectly through the centre from front to back. This line will be used as a guide to measure the positions of the legs and back supports and it must be retained throughout the construction of the chair.

Mark the position of the saddling on the seat and use a craft knife with a curved blade to carefully carve the saddling. (Reference to a life-sized Windsor chair will make this obvious.) Score a shallow groove around the circumference of the seat with a craft knife and define the groove with a riffler file. Sand the top of the seat thoroughly, rounding off the edges on both top and underside.

Cut the crest rail with a fret-saw from the pattern and sand thoroughly, rounding off the top edge to a smooth curve. Turn four legs, three stretchers and two back stands as shown on the pattern (see pp24–5). Remember that the tops of the legs and both ends of the stands should be extended sufficiently to peg into the seat and crest rail, and the stretchers into the legs.

The back sticks can be turned on a lathe, but it is easier to whittle them from $\frac{1}{16}$in square wood with a craft knife and sandpaper. Make five back sticks as shown on the pattern (remember to add sufficient length for pegging).

Using the guideline, carefully mark the positions of the legs on the underside of the seat and the back stands and sticks on the top of the seat. Refer to the pattern and drill

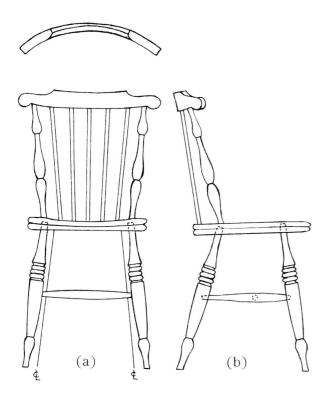

angled holes in the underside to receive the legs. Drill holes into the top to receive the back stands and sticks.

Mark the position of the centre stick on the underside of the crest rail, then mark evenly spaced positions of the other sticks to each side. Drill holes in the crest rail to receive the sticks.

Glue the back stands into the seat and the crest rail to the top of the back stands. If necessary, ease the back stands gently so that they are symmetrical. When this is thoroughly dry, the sticks are sprung into position. Locate the sticks in the chair seat, then gently bend and ease the tops into the crest rail.

Glue the front legs into the seat. Mark and drill holes for the stretchers in the front legs and back legs. Drill holes in the side stretchers for the centre stretchers. Glue the side stretchers into the front and back legs and the back legs into the seat as one operation. Apply a little glue to the holes in the side stretchers and ease the centre stretcher into place. The chair was finished with a coat of walnut stain and French polish, sanded gently and waxed.

It is worth saying to anyone making a chair of this type for the first time that if the result is less than perfect, chairs are probably the most difficult pieces to make because of the multifarious compound angles involved. Do not be disheartened; you will learn, largely by the mistakes in the early efforts, how to make good chairs.

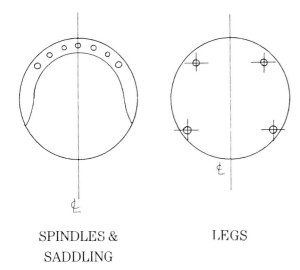

SPINDLES &
SADDLING

LEGS

Fig 48 PATTERN FOR THE CHAIR

CHEST-OF-DRAWERS · To make the carcase of the chest, cut two sides, a back, an under-top and a bottom from the pattern. You will also need approximately 18in of $3/32$ x $1/4$in wood to make the drawer runners (Fig 49, p70).

Mark and cut grooves for the drawer runners and back on the sides as shown on the pattern, using the shaper table (or a craft knife, metal rule and watchmaker's 'chisel'). Cut a $1/4$in long groove on the underside of the under-top to receive the top-drawer divider. Cut rabbets in the back edges of the under-top and bottom to receive the back.

Assemble the sides, back, bottom and under-top, clamping the pieces together as the glue dries.

Cut three pieces for each drawer runner and glue into place, in the grooves in the sides of the carcase as shown in Fig 49. Note that the top-drawer runner has a groove to correspond with the under-top.

Cut and fit a divider in the top-drawer space.

Cut the top as shown on the pattern and use the shaper table to cut the curved edge on the front sides. Glue the top in place, lining up the back edge with the carcase and clamp until the glue dries. To make the base, cut a 6in length of wood $5/16$ x $1/8$in. Use the shaper table to cut the curved edge as shown on the diagram. Cut and assemble three pieces with mitred corners as shown. Glue the base to the bottom of the carcase.

Cut and assemble three large and two small drawers using Method 2 as described on pp23–4.

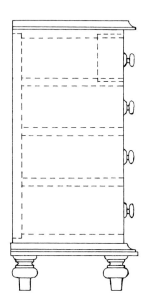

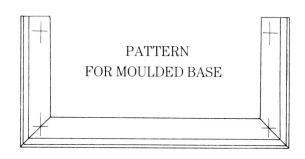

PATTERN
FOR MOULDED BASE

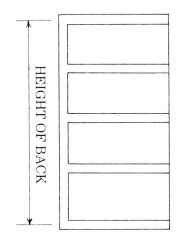

HEIGHT OF BACK

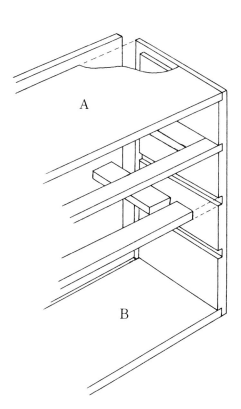

A

B

Showing placement of dados and
rabbet on right hand side.

Note that the back edges of the
parts A & B are rabbeted to
receive the back

Fig 49 PATTERN AND ASSEMBLY FOR THE CHEST-OF-DRAWERS

Plate 12 CONTENTS OF THE DOLLMAKER'S WORKROOM

The drawer knobs and bun feet are turned in boxwood. Any similar pale hardwood may be used, but pine is not recommended as it will not take the crisp definition required. The knobs are turned with small shanks which are glued into holes drilled in the drawer fronts. The bun feet are simply butted and glued to the base (see p24 for notes on turning). The chest of-drawers was finished with a light coat of thinned light-oak stain and one coat of French polish, sanded and waxed. This finish is best applied before the drawer knobs are glued in place.

ACCESSORIES · The corner unit is filled with an assortment of doll-making tools and materials. On top of the cupboard are bolts of felt and white cotton-lawn. These are strips of fabric, the edges of the cotton sealed with Fraycheck, wrapped tightly around lengths of fine dowelling. The felt bolt is 3in wide and the white lawn is 2¼in wide. On the top shelf are a set of plastic bowls, cut from pre-formed plastic packaging. These were cut from a bubble pack which contained a doll's plastic tea-set.

The tiny books are made with typing-paper pages and covered with pictures cut from doll magazine advertisements for books. The packet of Milliput is a small block of wood, painted white with a glued-on Milliput label from an advertisement. The tiny doll's head is from Christina Wakeham and the mug from Carol Lodder (see list of stockists, p177). On the next shelf are more books, a packet of tiny wax chips scraped from a candle and wrapped in polythene and a roll of tracing-paper. The plastic beaker is a bottle cap and the tiny china doll is from Recollect. The next shelf holds a packet of Super Sculpy, made like the Milliput, and more books. The coloured pencils are cut from cocktail sticks, coloured with felt pen in a small glass beaker. The pots of paint are the ends sawn off felt-pen casings and finished with tiny labels cut from a magazine. The other glass-beaker holds stringing hooks made from paperclips, stuffing tools cut from cocktail sticks and eye-sizer tools – glass-headed dressmaker's pins. On the shelf below are polythene bags of toy stuffing, a hank of shirring elastic (for stringing dolls) and two doll covers – pictures cut from magazines and folded. The bottom shelf holds a matchbox tray full of mohair-scrap 'wigs', a small bolt of stockinette fabric, a roll of fine vilene, a roll of very thin foam, another book and several tiny sheets of fine sandpaper.

The noticeboard is a piece of cork tile, framed with thin wood-strip with mitred corners. A collection of doll pictures and fabric scraps are glued to it. The calendar is a magazine cut-out.

The chest-of-drawers contains a selection of fine laces and ribbons wound on cards (see Chapter 7, p89) and small pieces of folded fabric; each drawer is filled. The basket contains folded pieces of printed cotton fabrics. The cane wastepaper basket, filled with crumpled paper and scraps, is from Mini Mansions (see list of stockists, p176).

DOLLS · The dolls (see Fig 50) are made from 1cm diameter whitewood beads and pipecleaners. Bend the pipe-cleaner in half and glue the folded end into the hole in the bead. Cut to length and bend the bottom ¼in forward for the feet. Cut the arm length and glue it to the body. Bind the body with surgical tape (available from chemist shops) to hold everything in place. To thicken the doll's legs, dip them in Gesso – liquid plaster which is available from art shops – and leave to dry. Paint the arms and legs with flesh-colour paint and paint boots or socks and shoes as you wish. Dot the eyes onto the face with a fine-point pen. Knickers are made from a scrap of lace, glued around the body and caught between the legs. The dolls' dresses are made of ribbon – ¼in, ½in and 1in wide – all in matching ribbons. Roll short lengths of ¼in ribbon and glue around the arms to make sleeves. Fold a 1in length of ½in ribbon, cut a neck hole and slash open the back; glue onto the doll, over the sleeves as a bodice. Cut a 3in length of 1in-wide ribbon, fold along the length to make two tiers and press. Blanket stitch the back seam. With tiny stitches, gather along the fold, pull up to fit the doll and slip stitch to the doll's waist. Trim with a tiny ribbon bow. Make the hair from embroidery silk, stitching through about a dozen strands to make a parting and gluing the hair onto the doll's head with UHU when the doll is dressed. Make another tiny bow and glue to the doll's hair.

These dolls may be made smaller or larger as you wish, depending on the size of bead you use for the head. The dolls illustrated are 1½in tall. (See also the pattern and instructions given for the tiny felt doll shown in Chapter 2, p45).

The dolls on the chest-of-drawers and the sewing-machine are from The Mulberry Bush (see list of stockists, p176). The doll seated on the floor is from the local toyshop and similar small plastic dolls are also sold as cake decorations.

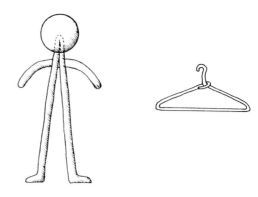

Fig 50 PATTERNS FOR TINY DOLL AND COAT-HANGER

The coat-hangers (Fig 50) are made from paperclips, bent with pliers. The green dress is made from silk ribbon, trimmed with fine lace, in the same way as the dolls' dresses described above. The dress is put on the hanger and finished with a piece of narrow ribbon folded around the hanger to simulate a collar, and a large bow. The matching hat is made from short lengths of ribbon and lace, the short ends seamed. One long edge is gathered and pulled up tightly to form a cap, which is trimmed with a bow. The scissors are from Wentways Miniatures and the pinking shears and tape measure are from Polly Flinders (see list of stockists, p177). The tiny cotton-reels are turned on the lathe and wound with cotton thread.

The doll-maker is a porcelain doll made from a kit from Christina Wakeham (see list of stockists, p177). The doll has a dark brown mohair wig and her spectacles are from Wentways Miniatures. She wears blue needlecord trousers and a red, printed cotton shirt. Patterns and instructions for dolls' clothes are given in Chapter 7, pp94, 96–7, 100–1. The doll's navy-blue sweater was knitted by Isobel Hockey who has provided the pattern and the introduction to miniature knitting given here.

MINIATURE KNITTING

You need to enjoy knitting, have good eyesight or a good magnifier, a reasonable amount of patience and a good basic knowledge of the craft.

EQUIPMENT · Where suppliers' addresses are given, please send a stamped addressed envelope for details of prices, etc.

Needles The best length for comfortable mini-knitting is 6–8in. Double-pointed pairs of sizes 16 and 18 needles are available from: The Thorn Press, The Old Vicarage, Godney Wells, Somerset, BA5 1RX.
Crochet hooks For crocheting round edges, use a .75 hook, which is available from branches of the John Lewis Partnership.
Wool You will need 1-ply or its near equivalent. 1-ply cobweb lace wool in white only is available from: Jamieson & Smith, 90 North Road, Lerwick, Shetland Isles, ZE1 0PQ.

Another possibility is Medici embroidery wool, minimally thicker than the cobweb wool and available from any good specialist needlework shop or by post from Mace & Nairn, 89 Crane Street, Salisbury, Wiltshire, SP1 2PY. It comes in a wide range of pleasant colours and is available in both small skeins and large 1¾oz (50g) hanks.

Cotton DMC lace-making cotton, size 70, is available in large balls in ecru and white and small balls in a limited range of colours by post from Mace & Nairn or from good needlework shops.

Buttons Tiny beads can be used and are available from Sunday Dolls (see list of stockists, p177), as is narrow silk ribbon for ties and trimming.

KNITTING · It is not easy to produce a basic knitting pattern that will work every time. The slightest variation in tension, needles or yarn radically changes the size. A good way to get the feel of knitting small is to use a pattern for a knitted outfit for a small doll. Make it, using your finest needles and yarn. The finished article most likely will not fit any particular doll as the proportions will be different when reduced in this way. However, it can now be used to adapt the pattern – ie, to work out where more or less stitches, extra rows and so on are needed. As you work, make a note of what you are doing.

It is a good idea to use light colours at first as they are easier on the eye and make it easier to pick up a dropped stitch. It is possible to do this using a crochet hook if the knitting is plain. It is possible also to work back and rectify a mistake, although this is a very stressful and tedious occupation. It is usually simpler and quicker to scrap the whole thing and start again. If you are working an eight-row lace pattern for a shawl or bedspread, it is a good idea to count the stitches as you knit each wrong side row, which is usually a plain purl row. The wrong number of stitches indicates an error. It is best to knit little and often and preferably when you are not too tired. A good idea is to have two pieces of work on the go at once, one on size 18 needles, the other on size 16 needles so that you can switch to working with larger needles when your eyes are tired. Spread a large, clean handkerchief on your lap before starting to keep your work clean. Crochet around the neck edge to give a neat finish. You can also crochet a loop for a button fastening instead of making a buttonhole. Crochet a lacy edging on shawls to give an attractive finish. This is easier and quicker than the knitted variety.

One advantage of these small garments is the small amount of wool they use. Joins must be avoided as much as possible because of bulk. All ends must be carefully darned in. When you use an extra colour, let the end hang at the side to be either darned in or caught in along the seam when sewing up, for which the oversew stitch is best. You must not start or finish with a knot. When you start, lay the end of the thread along the seam and oversew back over it. To finish, take a few extra stitches back along the seam, then weave the needle carefully through a couple of stitches.

Wash the knitting when you have finished, using lukewarm water and liquid soap, then gently pull to shape and leave to dry on a double thickness of white kitchen paper spread on a cake cooling-rack. Do not leave natural wool garments in sunlight – white ones will turn yellow. When the garments are dry, give a gentle press, preferably on the wrong side, with a warm to hot iron and a dry cloth. A cloth is not needed to press cotton garments, but don't be heavy handed or let the iron linger or you will scorch your work.

DOLL'S SWEATER PATTERN

Materials Pair of size 18 needles; a .75 crochet hook (optional); 2 skeins Medici embroidery wool; small bead for button.

Size To fit a lady doll approximately 5⅝in tall. The size can be adjusted by casting on more or less stitches and working more or less rows.

Abbreviations k=knit; p=purl; st=stitch; sts=stitches; beg=beginning; ss=stocking stitch (1 row k, 1 row p); yon=yarn over needle; tog=together.

METHOD · Cast on 24 sts.
Work 5 rows in k1, p1 rib, working into the back of the sts on the first row.
Work 20 rows in ss.
Cast on 14 sts at beg of next 2 rows.
Work 10 rows in ss.
Next row: k21, leave these sts on a safety-pin, cast off 10, k to end.
Work 7 rows as on the last 21 sts.
Next row: Cast on 5, k to end.
Next row: p to last 2 sts. yon, k2 tog, then, keeping a 2 st k border at neck edge, work 9 rows in ss.
Next row: Cast off 14 sts, p to last 2 sts, k2. Break off wool, leave these sts on a safety-pin.
Put the other group of sts back on needle, rejoin wool to sleeve end and work 7 rows in ss.
Next row: Cast on 7 sts, k2, p to end. Keeping the 2 st k border at neck edge, work 10 rows in ss.
Next row: Cast off 14 sts, k to last 2 sts, put the sts on the safety-pin onto a spare needle. Place the first 2 sts on the left-hand needle over the last 2 sts from the right-hand needle; k tog the first left-hand st and the second to last right-hand st, then k tog the second left-hand st and the last right-hand st. This will form an overlap with the buttonhole on top. Now k to end of row.
Work 19 rows in ss, then k1, p1 rib for 5 rows. Cast off in rib.

Cuffs Pick up and k15 sts at the end of each sleeve. Rib 5 rows. Cast off in rib.

To make up Press lightly on wrong side. Darn in loose ends. Oversew side and sleeve seams together. Work a row of single crochet around the neck edge if desired. Sew on bead to correspond to buttonhole.

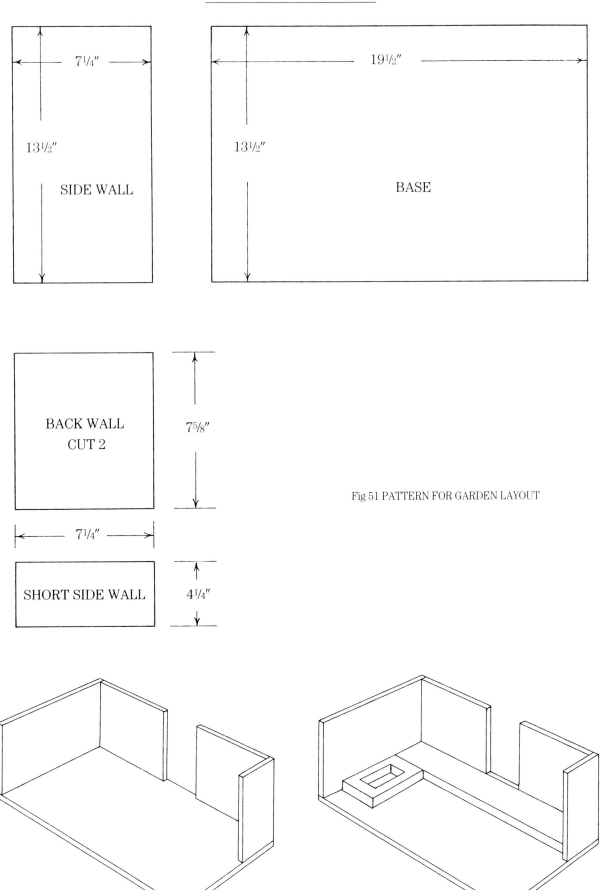

7¼″

13½″

SIDE WALL

19½″

13½″

BASE

BACK WALL
CUT 2

7⅝″

7¼″

SHORT SIDE WALL

4¼″

Fig 51 PATTERN FOR GARDEN LAYOUT

(a)

(b)

Fig 52 CONSTRUCTION OF GARDEN LAYOUT

6
THE SECRET GARDEN

As the interest in miniatures grows, the imagination moves outside the house and into the garden. This project re-creates the type of walled garden found around many old English houses – sheltered and peaceful, full of the scents and colours of a warm summer afternoon.

The garden is a complete project, but you can adapt the ideas and techniques to landscape around a dolls' house, or to design your own garden.

The garden is built on a plywood base, assembled with wood glue and 1in veneer pins. The terrace is built up with balsa wood and the bricks and paving stones are made from self-hardening clay – we have used Das, available from art and craft shops.

LAYOUT · To make the basic layout, cut the pieces shown on the pattern in Fig 51 from ³⁄₈in thick plywood. Glue and pin the long side wall onto the base. Glue and pin the short side wall onto the base, and the back walls onto the base and to the side walls (Fig 52a). Sand the outside thoroughly – do not sand the inside as the slightly rough surface will ensure that the bricks adhere well. If you wish to cover the underside of the base with felt or flocked paper, do it at this stage.

Make the terrace from balsa wood – this may be simply a 4in wide piece, 1in thick cut to fit, or more cheaply made up in pieces using ¼in thick balsa on a framework of scrap wood (see Fig 55a).

Cut the back terrace and glue in place. Cut a small piece of balsa to fit the gap to extend the terrace between the two back walls. Cut the side terrace and use a fret-saw to cut out the area for the pond. Glue the side terrace in place (Fig 52b).

BRICKS · To make the bricks, terracotta-coloured Das is most suitable. You will need two large packets to make the walls, steps and tiles as shown in the photographs.

Roll out the clay on a large flat surface with an old rolling-pin until it is approximately ⅛in thick and cut rectangles 1in larger than each wall to allow for shrinkage – one piece for each wall. With a pointed tool, eg a stylus or small knitting-needle, and a ruler, mark out the bricks (Fig 53). Draw evenly spaced lines in the clay to mark each row of bricks, then define the individual bricks. This takes time and patience and you may find the clay beginning to dry as you work. Brush water over areas which need it to keep the clay damp as you mark the bricks. When the four pieces (one for each wall) are marked, leave them on a flat surface to dry. Roll out and mark two brick piers to go on either side of the gate. These may be a little thicker than ⅛in, but take care that the brick pattern matches on both piers. The piers are 1in wide. Leave the piers to dry. The front of the terrace is faced with brick, made in the same way as the walls. Roll out the clay and cut strips to fit the front of the terrace. Divide this width into even brick courses – we found that three courses fitted perfectly. Mark the individual bricks to match the walls and leave the strips to dry.

Fig 53 PATTERN FOR MARKING OUT BRICKS

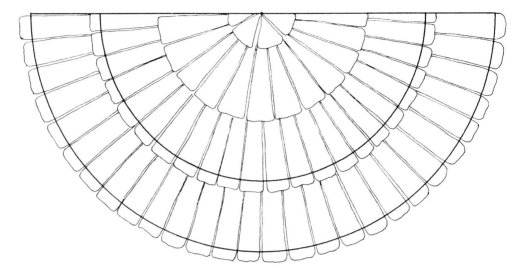

Fig 54 PATTERN FOR THE BRICKED STEPS

TILES · To make the tiles to go on top of the walls, roll out the clay to approximately ⅛in thick and mark it out in ¾in squares. This may be done as one large piece which will later be cut into strips.

STEPS · To make the steps, cut the pattern (Fig 54) in ⅜in thick balsa wood. Glue the top step to the bottom with UHU. Roll out the clay to ⅛in thick, brush the steps with water to dampen them, then cover the steps with clay. Smooth the clay over the steps, pressing it into the corners and trimming away the excess with a knife. Check that the clay is bonded to the balsa wood and trimmed evenly at the edges. Mark the bricks as shown in Fig 54 and leave to dry.

PAVING · The paving stones are made of grey Das — one packet will be sufficient. Roll out the clay ⅛in thick, to a piece more than large enough to cover the area of the terrace. Mark out the paving stones in 1in squares and leave to dry. As the pieces of brick and paving stone dry out, turn them over from time to time and, if they begin to warp excessively, press them under a weight. Drying will probably take two or three days but can be speeded up by using a hair-dryer. When all the clay pieces are thoroughly dry, sand them gently with fine-grade abrasive paper and remove all traces of dust.

ASSEMBLY · Glue the sheets of brick to the walls by smearing UHU glue all over the back of the clay and pressing it firmly in place to the wood. Check that each piece fits well, trim any overhang with a craft knife and fill any gaps with wet clay smoothed in with a finger, redefining the bricks if necessary. Glue the brick piers to either side of the gateway, gluing the pier on top of the brick facing with UHU and checking that the outside edges of both pieces line up. Glue the brick strips to the front of the terrace, trimming or filling gaps if necessary as for the walls.

The ends of the walls and the edges of the gateway are faced with damp clay strip. Paint water onto these edges with a brush to thoroughly dampen them. Roll out the clay to ⅛in thick and cut strips to fit the edges. Smooth the clay strips in place and mark the bricks to line up with the walls, then leave to dry.

Dampen the top edge of the walls and roll a thin 'sausage' of clay to fit all the way around. Press this clay roll in place on top of the walls and brush the clay with more water. Cut the tiles into strips and place them on top of the walls. Pressing firmly, angle the front edge downwards and 'bed' the tiles in the clay on top of the wall. Trim away any excess clay with a knife and smooth a flat back edge. Tiles will need to be cut into triangles to fit into the corners. The clay 'sausage' has now become a triangular fillet between the top of the wall and the tiles, and should be left to dry. Cut and fit the paving stones around the pool and along the terrace. Glue them in place with UHU so that they overhang the front edge of the terrace slightly. Fill gaps and between the gateposts with pieces of paving stone cut to fit. Check the walls and paving stones critically, patch and fill gaps or spaces if necessary with wet clay smoothed in with the finger, and leave this to dry thoroughly before painting.

PAINTING · Although the walls are terracotta and the paving stones grey, they will need to be painted for realism. Both poster colour and acrylic are suitable, but they must be used fairly thickly as watery colours simply 'disappear' into the clay. Begin by giving the walls and tiles a thick undercoat of dark brick colour and the paving stones a thick undercoat of dark grey. The paint should be worked well into all the cracks. Allow this undercoat to dry thoroughly, then paint the bricks and tiles and, when these are dry, paint the paving stones. When you paint the walls, paint the steps at the same time to ensure that the colours are similar.

THE SECRET GARDEN

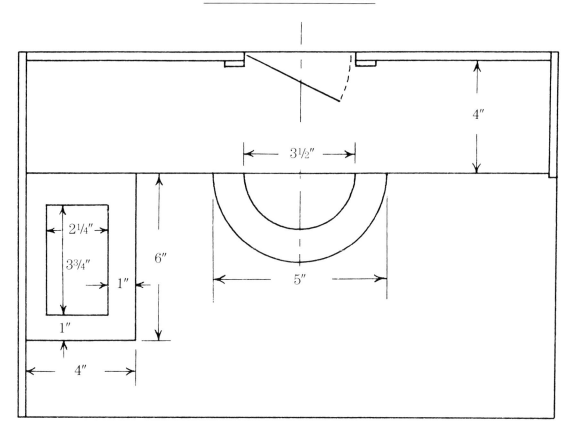

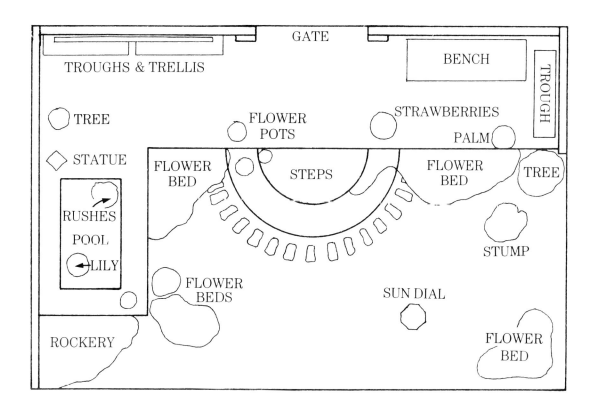

Fig 55 PLANS FOR GARDEN LAYOUT

Plate 13 THE SECRET GARDEN

Plate 14 THE SECRET GARDEN

BENCH · We made the garden bench of oak, but any similar hardwood may be used (Fig 57). The bench is made using mortise and tenon joints which can be cut using the shaper table or a craft knife, metal rule and watchmaker's 'chisel' as described on p14. Care should be taken to ensure that the joints are marked accurately and that joints on both sides of the bench correspond exactly.

The two sides of the bench are made first. Cut two back legs, two front legs and four side stretchers. Carefully cut the mortises and tenons and two grooves to receive the arms. Glue the side stretchers between the front and back legs and clamp until they are dry. Check that the construction is square and both legs are parallel.

To join the sides, cut two back rails and the front rail. Cut mortises to fit the tenons in the legs. Use the shaper table to cut a groove in the underside of the top rail as shown in Fig 57a to receive the back slats.

Glue the three rails between the two sides and allow to dry, checking that the construction is square and all four feet rest flat on the work surface.

Mark the positions of the seven back slats on both top and bottom rails. Cut the slats as shown and glue in place. The slats are pushed into the groove in the top rail and butted to the bottom rail.

Cut five seat slats and, using the notched joint as shown in Fig 57b, fit these between the side stretchers. Space the slats evenly and glue in place. Cut a similar slat and fit centrally between the bottom stretchers.

Cut a pair of arms and glue them into the back legs and onto the front legs. When these are dry, drill holes ¹⁄₁₆in in diameter through the arms into the front legs. Cut pegs to fit and glue in place.

As this piece of furniture is designed for a garden, it was neither stained nor polished, but left as natural wood.

Glued into the right-hand corner to overhang the bench are several sprays of dried flowers, the sprays chosen to give some colour variation in shades of light to dark pink. The flowers are glued where they touch the wall, to hold them firmly in place. Beside the bench are two more plant troughs filled with clumps of flowers like those on the other side of the terrace. On the bench is a cane trug from C & D Crafts (see list of stockists, p177) and a straw boater from 'Fifi la Belle' (see Chapter 7, p92).

The little tree (in a pot from Carol Lodder) is a model landscape tree, as is the larger one on the right. Clumps of dried flowers in reindeer moss in pots stand on the terrace with a strawberry pot from The Singing Tree (see list of stockists, p176).

(a)

(b)

Fig 57 PATTERN AND ASSEMBLY FOR THE GARDEN BENCH

MADAME FIFI'S FASHION EMPORIUM

This project has been designed for anyone who loves the fripperies and fancies of Edwardian fashion. Both the shop and the furniture are made from kits, so even those who have never worked with wood should have no difficulty making them and full instructions are given for the gowns and hats and all the little items which stock the shop.

SHOP KITS · Several of the specialist suppliers now offer shops (and dolls' houses) in kit form at very reasonable prices, which makes building a shop a simple matter with only the minimum of tools. We chose this kit from Thames Valley Craft (see list of stockists, p176) because it is simple, spacious and the design makes it suitable for a wide range of trades. The kit is made of plywood, and all the pieces are pre-cut and need only to be sanded and assembled. The instructions are clear and concise and the kit is well made. We have 'customised' our shop kit by adding the curved fascia boards at the top of the windows to give the shop an Edwardian look. The instructions call for the roof to be fixed in place, but as we preferred to make it removable, we have screwed pegs to the walls in the four corners of the shop which fit into holes drilled in the roof (see Plates 15–16).

The following notes are offered to anyone using a shop (or dolls' house) kit for the first time. As soon as you have the kit, check it carefully against the parts list to be sure that it is complete. Check that none of the pieces is warped and if any are, return the kit for an exchange (explaining why) because warped pieces will not produce a good result. Despite the most careful storage and packing, timber is susceptible to changes in temperature, etc, and it is beyond the supplier's control to guarantee that a kit will not warp. Any reputable supplier will gladly exchange a kit for this reason.

Read the instructions carefully from beginning to end and make sure that you understand them fully before starting construction. Always dry-fit the pieces together as you go along, before assembling with glue. Even when the instructions call only for glue, the larger parts should be glued *and* pinned for extra strength.

Kits are usually supplied rough-sanded and will need to be thoroughly sanded before any finish is applied. Sand first with medium-grade, then with fine-grade, abrasive paper.

Remember that the kit is only the beginning of the project. How you choose to 'customise', decorate and stock it is entirely up to you. Consider using the brick-making technique described on p75, or the timbering described on p126 as possibilities for the outside. Consider glazing bars, leaded windows or shaped fascias like those on Fifi la Belle. The decorating scheme should be appropriate for the type of trade your shop represents. For example, an Old Curiosity Shop might have leaded windows, ceiling beams and a planked floor.

DECORATING · We decorated the exterior with coffee-coloured silk emulsion paint and black Humbrol enamel gloss. We found it easier to paint the fronts and decorate the interior of the shop before the fronts were hinged in place (see pp9 and 12 for full details on decorating). The shop sign was painted with gold enamel paint onto a strip of black card cut to fit and glued in place after painting. If you prefer, Letraset may be used either directly onto the fascia board or on cardboard.

The interior of the shop is papered with dolls' house wall-paper and carpeted with flocked paper. The front of the base is papered with a floor-tile pattern. We fitted commercial skirting-board (from Hobby's – see list of stockists p175) of stained mahogany, glued in place after the walls and floor were papered.

The windows were edged with strips of gilt paper, cut from a band used to decorate cakes and glued in place with UHU and lace curtains, threaded onto fine brass rods, were hung from tiny eyes screwed into the back edges of the windows.

The shop is lit with 'gas lamps' and a copper-tape wiring kit from Thames Valley Craft. The wires were fed through holes drilled in the walls and the copper tape was run on the outside of the shop.

FURNITURE KITS · The furniture in our shop is all made from kits from Blackwells of Hawkwell (see list of stockists, p175), chosen from an extensive range of pieces suitable for any house or shop. This was the first time we have used kits, and we were pleasantly surprised by the quality of the finished items. For anyone who finds working with wood daunting, or whose space, time or tools are limited, these kits are an excellent way to make miniatures. The time-consuming measuring and cutting are all done for you and the kit needs only to be sanded, assembled and finished to produce a piece of furniture at a fraction of the cost of a commercial piece. For the absolute beginner, we would recommend making a few kits as a good introduction to making miniatures, and which would give you some experience and almost inevitably good results. Once you have made up a few kits, you will find the plans and methods in the book easy to follow and will probably be keen to make your own pieces 'from scratch'. We offer the following tips to anyone using a kit for the first time.

Check that all the pieces shown on the parts list are complete. Read the instructions from beginning to end and be sure you understand them before beginning construction. The pre-cut pieces will need to be fine-sanded, but this must be done carefully to avoid changing the dimensions of the pieces so that they no longer fit together properly.

As far as possible, leave the final sanding until the piece is completed. Before assembly, sand each piece lightly with 320-grit abrasive paper. Wherever possible, use the abrasive wrapped around a small sanding block to avoid rounding any edges. Always dry-fit the pieces together as you go along before assembling with glue.

As wood stain will not take over wood glue, small pieces should be stained before assembly – if you wish, all pieces may be stained before assembly. Any type or colour of spirit-based wood stain can be used, applied with either a cloth or brush as described on pp24–5, which also gives instructions for painting furniture and can be applied to kits.

If you dislike the fabric supplied for upholstery, change it for a fabric of your own choice, but use something of a similar weight and texture. When you have made a few kits, you might like to try 'customising' kits, adding or omitting pieces to adapt the original design or using pieces from two kits to create an original piece of furniture.

DUMMIES · The body of the tailor's dummy (Fig 59) is carved in balsa wood. Cut a firm piece of balsa 1 x 1¼in and 3¼in long. Trace the patterns onto the front and sides of the balsa block. Use a fret-saw to cut the outline of the body. This shape will have square edges – use a craft knife to pare the corners into smooth curves. Work gradually from side to side to retain the symmetry. When you are satisfied with the shape, smooth the body with medium-grade sandpaper and finish with 320-grit abrasive paper. For the full-length dummy, mark the centre on the underside and drill a ¹/₁₂ diameter hole to receive the stand. (For the half-size dummy, the original balsa block is only 2½in long.)

To make the stand, prepare a 4in length of ¼in square wood (we used cherry) and chuck onto the lathe. Turn to

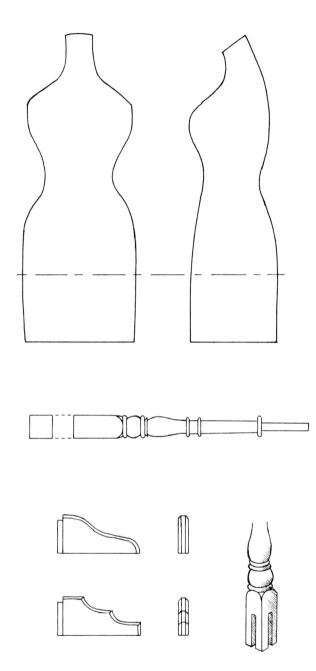

Fig 59 PATTERN FOR THE TAILOR'S DUMMY

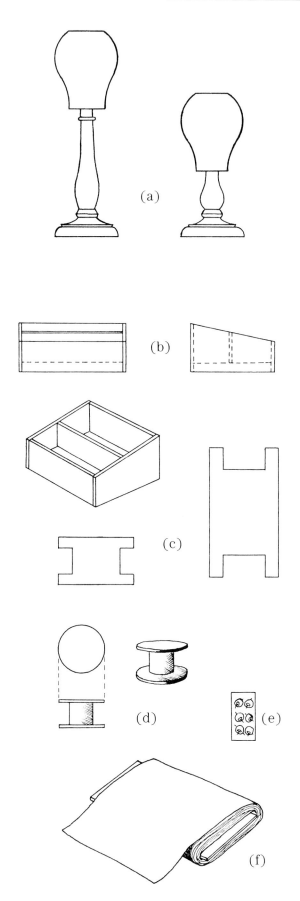

Fig 60 ACCESSORIES FOR THE FASHION EMPORIUM: (A) HAT-STAND; (B) DISPLAY BOX; (C) TRIMMINGS CARDS; (D) RIBBON REEL; (E) BUTTON CARD; (F) FABRIC BOLT

the pattern shown (see p87), leaving a length of square section wood at the top to support the piece, while the tenons are cut on the shaper table. Cut four feet (from either pattern) chamfering the top edges slightly. Cut the mortises to fit the tenons in the stand. Glue the feet into the stand and allow to dry. Dry-fit the stand into the body to ensure that it stands upright. Adjust the hole if necessary and stain and polish the stand before gluing it into the body. We left the body unpainted, because we liked this finish. Dummies may be bought from The Mulberry Bush (the tea gown is displayed on one – see list of stockists, p176).

HAT-STAND · The hat-stands are turned from ¾in diameter dowelling – we used a broom handle. For the taller stand, use a 3½in length, for the smaller, a 2½in length (Fig 60a).

Because of the diameter of these pieces, you will need to use the two- or four-pronged driver in the lathe. The stands were sanded smooth and given two coats of wax polish while they were still on the lathe.

As a simple alternative to the turned-wood hat-stand, a golf tee, up-ended with a small polystyrene ball pushed and glued onto the point, makes an effective stand. Spray-paint in any colour you choose, and, if necessary, fill the cup of the golf tee with clay or Plasticine for extra stability. Hats do look their best displayed on stands.

DISPLAY BOXES · To make the boxes, use ½in plywood (or cardboard) for the sides and ⅜in wood for the base (Fig 60b). Cut the base, front and back and glue the front and back to the outside of the base, ensuring that they are perfectly upright. Cut the sides and glue in place. Because of the fineness of the material, the sides should be cut slightly overlong and trimmed flush with a craft knife after they are glued in place. Cut the divider, glue the bottom edge and slip into place.

STOCKING THE SHOP

Stocking the shop is a matter of personal taste – you may prefer to sell only hats rather than general haberdashery – but whatever you choose to make, having the right tools and materials will make things much easier. Working in this scale is fiddly and does require patience, but anyone who has neat fingers and the basic sewing skills should have no difficulty in making the items described here.

MATERIALS · There is one supplier, Sunday Dolls (see list of suppliers, p177), who specialises in miniature haberdashery and the tools to make miniature fashions, and we recommend that you get their catalogue before embarking on this project. They supply all the fabrics, ribbons, laces, braids, straw, beads, feathers, etc, that you will need to stock the shop. Several of the stockists supply ready-made fashion items to supplement those you make, or you may prefer to stock your shop entirely with bought items.

TOOLS · If you plan to make your stock you will need the following tools. Small sharp scissors, fine dressmaker's needles (size 10 sharps), a sharp HB pencil and small ruler and a supply of thin white cardboard. Sunday Dolls supply Aileens tacky glue (a white glue which disappears as it dries) and a syringe to use it in, diluted with water. The glue syringe will allow you to apply tiny beads of glue exactly where you want them – this is much neater than using glue from a tube. A rosemaker tool and a bowmaker tool are also very useful.

ROSES · The rosemaker tool (Fig 61b) is a large darning needle, snapped halfway down the eye, set into a dowelling handle. Roses are made of fine silk ribbon, twisted and glued, six or eight times around the tool, the twisted or folded ribbon forming the petals. This is a knack, acquired with a little practice; early efforts may look like worm-casts, but perseverance will produce very pretty flowers, perfectly scaled to trim miniature hats and clothes. Roses may also be made with stems, to use in a vase, by cutting a short length of green florist's wire and gluing the first twist of ribbon around the top end of the wire. Continue folding and gluing the ribbon to form the petals of the rose as before. A tiny piece of green ribbon, twisted and glued around the stem, trimmed to shape, will make leaves.

BOWS · The bowmaker (Fig 61a) is simply four thin nails, or pins, knocked through a small block of wood, spaced ¼in, ½in and 1in apart. The ribbon is wound around two pins and half-knotted in the centre to form a perfect and secure bow, which is then eased off the pins. This enables you to make tiny bows, almost impossible to do by hand. Fig 61 shows both tools, but they can be bought from Sunday Dolls if you prefer not to make them.

One other useful item is Fraycheck – this is a colourless fluid which is painted onto fabric edges to prevent them fraying. Glue can be used in this way, but Fraycheck is better as it does not stiffen the fabric. You can use it straight from the bottle, but this tends to be a little clumsy; it is neater to paint it on with a small paint-brush.

FABRICS · To make the fabric bolts (Fig 60f), cut pieces of cardboard ⅝in wide x 1½in long. Cut pieces of lightweight fabric, 1½in wide and 6–8in long, squarely on the grain of the fabric. Fold both long sides to the middle so that the raw edges meet and press. Glue one end of the fabric to the card and wrap the length tightly around the card, securing the end with a little glue. Make bolts of fabric in lightweight cotton, plain colours and tiny prints, silk, brocade, lace, fine wool, needlecord and velveteen. Anything that will wrap neatly around the cards may be used, but any patterns must be tiny. (Our shop contains forty-five bolts of fabric.)

RIBBONS · To make the ribbon spools (Fig 60d), cut two circles of cardboard, ½in in diameter for each spool. Cut a slice of ¼in diameter dowelling, ¼in long, and glue the

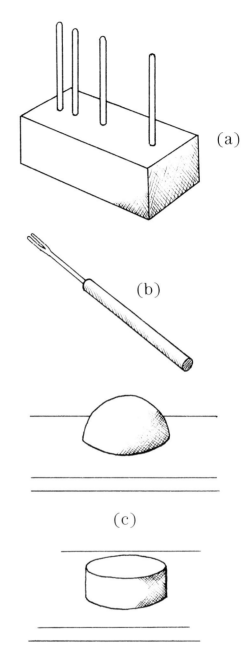

Fig 61 TOOLS FOR MAKING MINIATURE FASHIONS: (A) BOWMAKER; (B) ROSEMAKER; (C) HAT BLOCKS

card circles to each end. Cut the length of ribbon, glue one end to the dowelling and wrap the ribbon. Snip a tiny notch into one card end and pull the other end of the ribbon through the notch.

TRIMMINGS CARDS · To make the cards of trimmings (Fig 60c), cut the pattern in cardboard, glue the end of the trimming to the card, then wind the trimming, securing the end with a little glue. Use larger cards for laces and broderie Anglaise, smaller cards for narrow braids. Vary the amounts of fabric, ribbon and trimming you wind onto the cards so that they are not too uniform.

To make the cards of buttons (Fig 60e), cut cards ½ x ¼in and sew six tiny beads to each card.

Plate 15 MADAME FIFI'S FASHION EMPORIUM

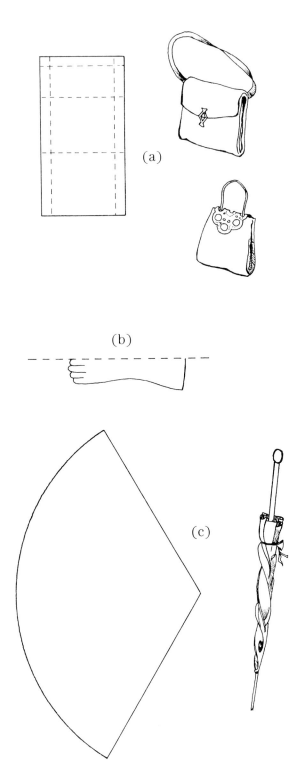

(a)

(b)

(c)

Fig 62 FASHION ACCESSORIES: (A) HANDBAGS; (B) GLOVES; (C) PARASOL

HATS · To make the straw hats, use tightly plaited raffia or miniature hat straw. Begin in the centre of the crown, coiling the straw and whipping the edges of each coil together with matching thread. Work outwards, shaping the hat into a shallow saucer-shape until it is the right size, then tuck the cut end of the straw inside and secure it. Make hat blocks (Fig 61c) to shape the finished hats by gluing half of a 1in diameter wooden bead or a ½in slice of 1in diameter dowelling to a small piece of plywood. Dampen the hat with water or steam it over the kettle and shape it on the hat block (leave it on the block until it is dry). If you use a wooden-bead block, the hat will have a dome-shaped crown, or a slice of dowelling will make a flat crown. You can speed the drying out – carefully – with a hot iron and if you want a flat brim, eg for a boater, iron the brim while the hat is on the block.

To make a felt hat, cut a piece of felt, roughly 3in square, and soak it thoroughly in wallpaper paste. Coat the hat block with a thin smear of vaseline to prevent the felt from sticking and drape the felt over the block. Use your fingers to mould the hat, smoothing out wrinkles and defining the shape. Leave the hat to dry on the block – do not iron it – then lift it off and trim the brim to shape with small sharp scissors. Felt hats made this way will have flat brims (straw being more pliant will only be completely flat if it is ironed.) Trim the hats with narrow ribbon or braid, feathers, artificial flowers and ribbon roses and bows. These tiny trimmings are neater glued in place, using Aileens tacky glue in a syringe.

HANDBAGS · To make the handbags, use very thin glove leather or fabric trimmed with jewellery findings. For the flap-over bag, cut a strip of leather, fold and glue the edges under on both long sides and one short side. Fold and glue the bag, then fold and glue the flap over a fine strip of leather cut to length for the handle (Fig 62a). Trim the front of the flap with a jewellery scrap for the catch. The second bag uses a bell cap, hammered flat for a decorative clasp. Cut a strip of leather, fold in and glue both long edges. Bend the hammered bell cap to fit over the top of the bag. Cut a length of fuse wire for the handle, bend it and push the ends through the bell cap and glue them into the bag. Glue the bell cap to the bag (Fig 62a).

GLOVES · To make the gloves, use fine glove leather. Cut a piece of leather approximately 3in long and 1½in wide. Fold the piece down the length and glue the two sides together. Cut the pattern against the folded edge of the leather, using small sharp scissors. Cut tiny pieces of leather and glue to the underside of each glove for the thumbs (Fig 62b).

PARASOLS · To make the parasols, use wooden toothpicks with small beads glued to one end for handles. Cut the cover from the pattern (Fig 62c) in lightweight fabric and glue the trimming to the curved edge. Seam the straight edges and push the point of the handle through the cover. Fold the cover around the handle and glue it in place. Trim with ribbon, bows or roses. The parasols are in an umbrella stand made from the lid of a tube of lipstick.

ACCESSORIES · The perfume bottles are small glass beads, glued together with a cut-down glass-headed pin through the centre. The tiny brass buckles and combs are from Wentways Miniatures (see list of stockists, p177). They are glued to display cards, covered in flocked Fablon. The belts are made of fine velvet ribbon with tiny buckles glued to one end. The shawl and scarves are rectangles cut from fabric, their edges sealed with Fraycheck. The fashion books are made with typing-paper pages and stiff paper covers, stapled together and filled with tiny pictures cut from magazines. The dress patterns are illustrations cut from the Laura Ashley catalogue, folded and glued into envelopes. The fan and the hat-box are from Polly Flinders (see list of stockists, p177). The bouquets are posies of artificial flowers (or ribbon roses made with stalks) with a short length of fine lace, gathered tightly around the stalks. The hat-pins are tiny beads and jewellery findings glued to dressmaker's pins.

One tailor's dummy is draped with silk, the others display miniature clothes. To drape the dummy, cut a length of silk and soak it in water. Pin one corner to the back of the shoulder and arrange the wet silk in graceful folds, pinning into the dummy to hold in place as the silk dries. When it is dry, remove the pins and glue where necessary. Trim with silk roses, a spray of feathers or whatever you please.

CLOTHES · Miniature dressmaking is fiddly, needs time and patience and some skill in needlework. If you prefer, all the dummies may be draped rather than dressed.

All garments are made in basically the same way, using lightweight fabrics and fine lace and ribbon trimmings. Iron the fabric, then draw the pattern onto the fabric with a sharp pencil. Paint the outline, all the way around each piece with Fraycheck, and allow it to dry. Cut out the pieces with small sharp scissors.

The method is the same whether you are making up the garment to go on a doll or a dummy and these instructions apply to all the clothes for dolls in this book, but you must check the fit on the individual doll and adjust the patterns if necessary. For patterns, see Figs 63–5.

Drawers Cut two pieces in fine cotton lawn. Glue lace trimming to both leg ends. Seam legs, then seam both pieces together from front to back through the crotch. Gather the top edge to fit the waist.

Petticoat Cut the pattern in fine cotton lawn. Glue lace trimming to the hem. Stitch the back seam and gather the top edge to fit the waist.

Skirt Cut the pattern, turn up a small hem, tack and press. Stitch the back seam, pull out the tacking and glue the hem in place. Gather the top edge to fit the waist. If the skirt is to be trimmed, glue the trimming in place before fitting the skirt. For the Edwardian effect, the gathering at the waist is concentrated at the back so that the skirt hangs straight in front and full at the back.

Chemise Cut the pattern in fine cotton lawn, cut the sleeves in lace. Whip stitch sleeves into armholes. Blanket stitch around the neckline with one strand of embroidery silk or sewing thread. Seam the sides from sleeve end through armhole to bottom edge. Gather sleeve ends and waistline with embroidery silk, pull up and fasten off or tie in a bow.

Bodice Cut one front, two backs and two sleeves. Stitch front to backs at the shoulder seams. Gather the sleeve heads to ease and set sleeves into the armholes. Stitch the side seams, from sleeve end through the armhole to the bottom edge. Turn up the bottom edge and press. Fit bodice and slip stitch the back opening closed. Glue trimming in place as required.

Tea gown Cut one piece from the pattern. Glue lace and ribbon trimming to the fronts and, slightly gathered, around the neck. Glue trimming to sleeve ends and hemline. Stitch the side seams from the sleeve ends to the hem. Gather the sleeves and waistline with very fine ribbon or embroidery thread, and tie in bows. The dressing-gown in the Edwardian bedroom is made from this pattern simply trimmed with fine picot braid, whip stitched around the edges and tiny whipped 'pin tucks' on the shoulders. The gown in the shop is trimmed lavishly with lace and ribbon and has a pleated frill at the hem. Pleating in this scale is most easily done with a pleater (from Sunday Dolls) which is a ridged rubber device, in which tiny pleats are set by ironing. The lace-over-fabric pleated frill is made in one piece, and stitched to the lower edge of the (shortened) gown.

Dresses on dummies hang better if there is a petticoat underneath. Trimmings are easier to do if the garment is put on the doll or dummy first and may be stitched or glued in place, although gluing is usually neater. Dolls can be supported on small doll stands if they will not stand by themselves.

The hats and clothes you make are a matter of personal taste, but if you want authenticity, it is worth spending some time with a good costume reference book. Each period had its own styles and colours, and though ours is Edwardian, you may prefer Victorian, modern or anywhere in between. If you enjoy making fashionable fripperies, but don't want to open a shop, consider making a market stall to display them on.

Overleaf:
Plate 16 INTERIOR OF THE FASHION EMPORIUM

Plate 17 CONTENTS OF THE FASHION EMPORIUM

SUNDAY MORNING IN THE POTTING SHED

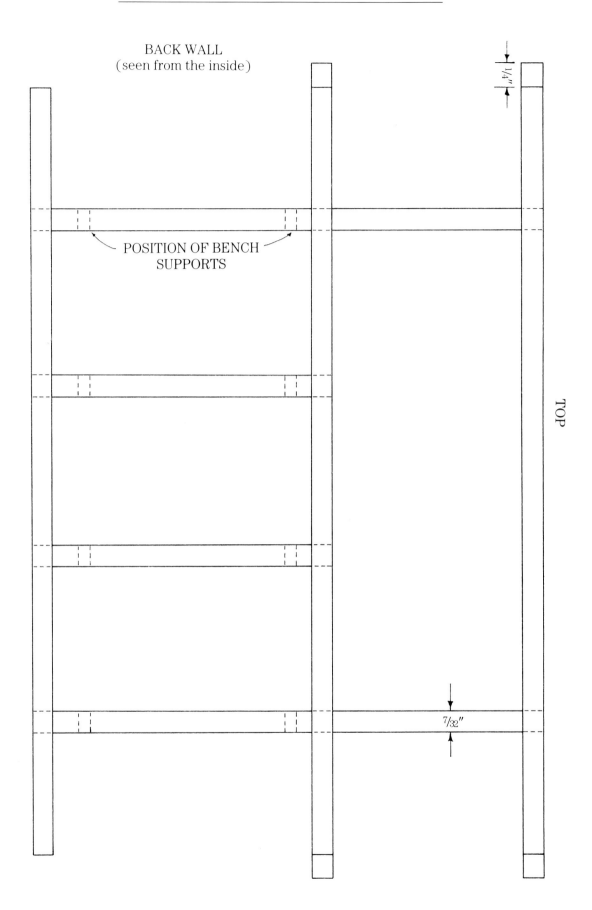

BACK WALL
(seen from the inside)

POSITION OF BENCH
SUPPORTS

1/4"

TOP

7/32"

Fig 66 PATTERN FOR POTTING-SHED BACK WALL

8
SUNDAY MORNING IN THE POTTING SHED

The potting shed is built as an authentic miniature. It stands on a wooden base designed to represent a corner of the garden and it is filled with all the odds and ends to be found in any potting shed. A mixture of bought and made items have been used as accessories for this project and the doll was made to commission by Sunday Dolls (see list of stockists, p177).

TO MAKE THE SHED

The potting shed is built in the same way as a life-size shed, by constructing a wooden framework and boarding this on the outside with wooden planks. The roof is tiled with wooden shingles (from Hobby's, see magazines, p175) on a framework of rafters and battens.

You will need approximately 15ft of 1/4 x 7/32in wood for the framework. This might be 1/4in square wood, planed to these dimensions, but we suggest that strips are cut from a sheet of 1/4in thick wood, eg pine or spruce, and used with the rough-cut finish. You will also need approximately 5ft of 1/8 x 7/32in wood for the rafters and outer framework and nine 3ft lengths of 1/16 x 3/8in wood-strip for the planking. The base is a 8½ x 6in piece of 1/8in thick plywood. The roof battens are made from very fine wood-strip (1/8 x 1/64in). We used commercial wooden shingles trimmed to 1 1/8in long. The shed is assembled with cross-halved joints and white wood glue.

Cut lengths of framework as shown on the pattern to make the back (Fig 66). Cut three long cross pieces, two long and two short upright pieces. Cut cross-half joints as shown in Figs 67a and b and glue and assemble the pieces. Note that the two upper cross pieces are notched at each end, the lower one is not, and is slightly shorter than the other two. Leave the assembly to dry. Mark in pencil the position of the work-bench supports as shown on the pattern.

Plate 18 THE POTTING SHED AND GARDEN BASE

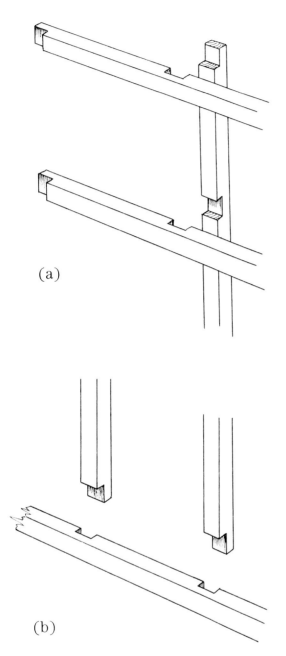

(a)

(b)

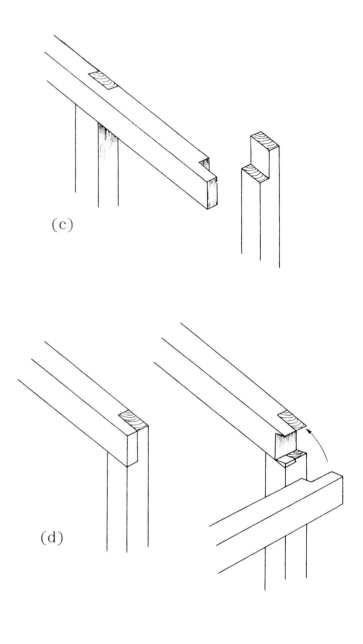

(c)

(d)

Fig 67 JOINTS USED TO ASSEMBLE POTTING SHED

To make the sides, cut lengths of framework as shown on the pattern. One side has five upright pieces and omits the small cross piece. The other side includes the small cross piece and omits the centre upright to make the door frame (see Fig 68).

The simplest way to assemble the sides is to use a tracing of the pattern as a guide. Cut joints and dry-assemble the bottom cross piece and the uprights. Place this assembly on the pattern, lining up the uprights and weight it to hold in place. Place the top apex pieces in position across the uprights and carefully mark the placement of the joints. Cut the joints and glue and assemble the sides. Leave to dry, then cut notches on the back edge of each side to receive the corresponding notches on the back assembly. Cut notches at the apex of each side for the ridge beam (Figs 67c and d).

SIDE
(viewed from the inside)

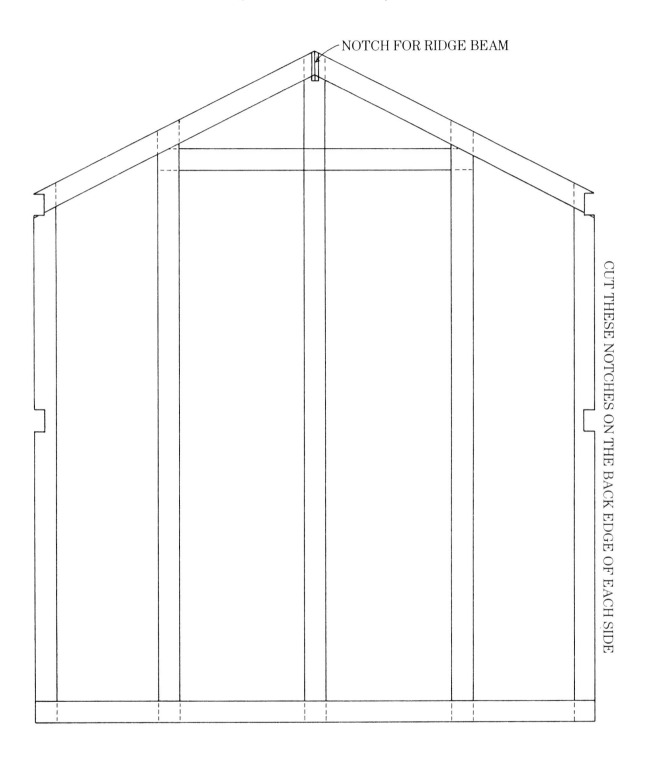

NOTCH FOR RIDGE BEAM

CUT THESE NOTCHES ON THE BACK EDGE OF EACH SIDE

Fig 68 PATTERN FOR POTTING-SHED SIDES

The shed is assembled so that it sits on top of the base. Glue and assemble the back and one side onto the base, clamping until dry. Glue and fit the second side in place, clamping until dry (Fig 69).

WINDOW · Assemble the window at this stage to allow maximum access. Cut and fit a frame of ³/₃₂in wood-strip flush with the inside edge of the window space. Cut 'glass' to fit the window space behind this frame. We used 1mm Lexan sheet, but any similar thin perspex would be suitable. Glue the 'glass' in place with a little UHU or similar glue. Cut and glue a second wood-strip frame outside the 'glass'. Cut and fit glazing bars to line up with the uprights of the framework and glue the bars to both the inside and the outside of the 'glass' (Fig 70).

WORK-BENCH · Make and fit the work-bench at this stage to allow maximum access. Use ⁷/₃₂in square wood for the frame and ³/₃₂in thick wood for the shelves. The bottom shelf is 1¼ x 8in and the top shelf is 1³/₈ x 8in. The shelves are supported on battens of wood ⅛in square.

Cut and glue the shelf support battens to the back wall on the positions marked for them. Assemble the frame (Fig 71) using cross-halved joints as shown in Fig 72. Cut notches in the front edge of the bottom shelf to correspond with and accommodate the frame uprights. Glue the frame in place behind the first uprights on both sides of the shed and allow to dry. Glue and fit the bottom shelf in placé to the frame and batten. Cut the top shelf and glue to the top of the frame and batten.

DOOR · Make and hang the door at this stage to allow maximum access. The door is made up of ¹/₁₆ x ³/₈in wood-strip planks, braced with ³/₃₂ x ³/₈in wood (Fig 73).

Cut and butt-joint eight 6in planks to make the door. When these are dry, trim to fit the door space. Cut two cross braces and one diagonal brace and glue to the inside of the door. Chamfer the edges of the cross braces on the opening side of the door to allow for smooth opening. Cut recesses to receive the hinges in the edge of the door at the cross braces and in the door frame. Hinge the door in place (see p12, for details).

Plate 19 SUNDAY MORNING IN THE POTTING SHED

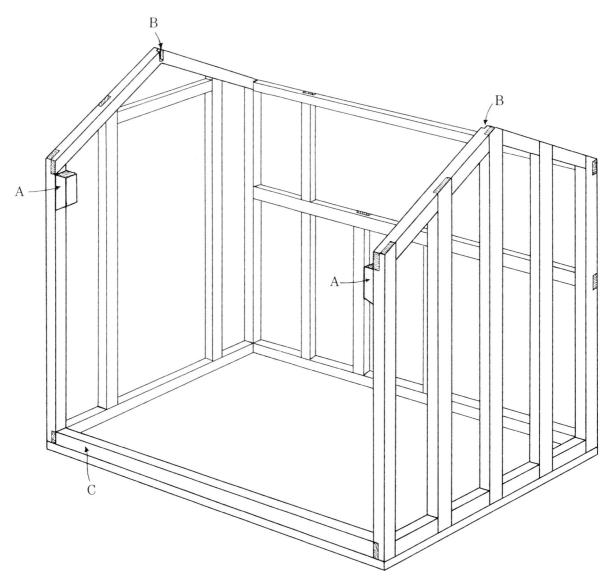

Fig 69 ASSEMBLED FRAMEWORK FOR THE POTTING SHED

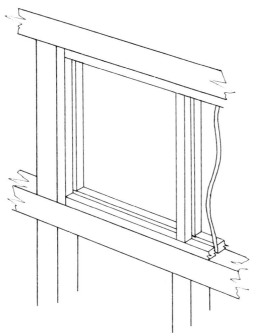

Fig 70 ASSEMBLY FOR WINDOW

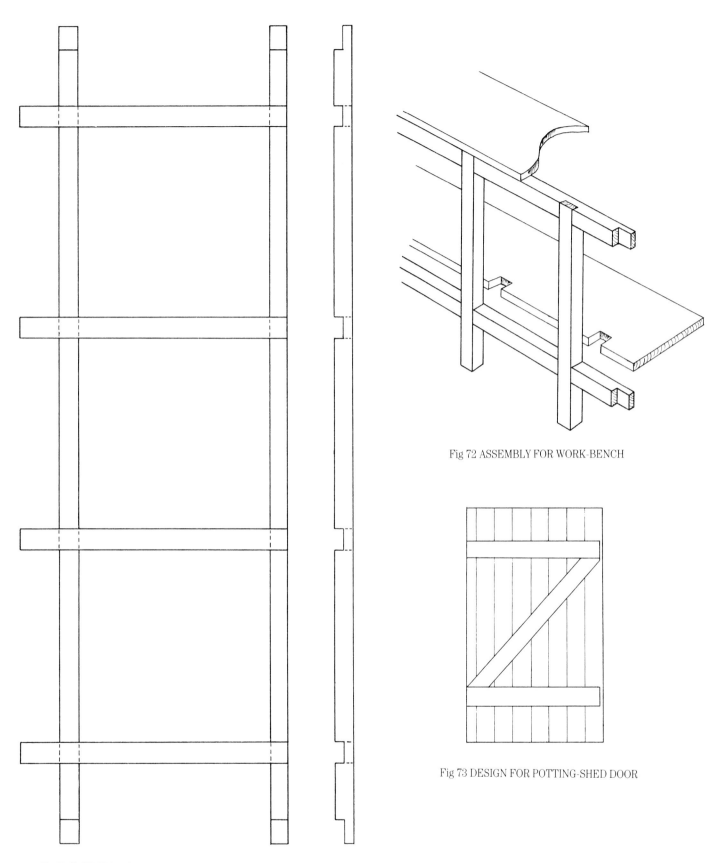

Fig 72 ASSEMBLY FOR WORK-BENCH

Fig 73 DESIGN FOR POTTING-SHED DOOR

Fig 71 PATTERN FOR WORK-BENCH

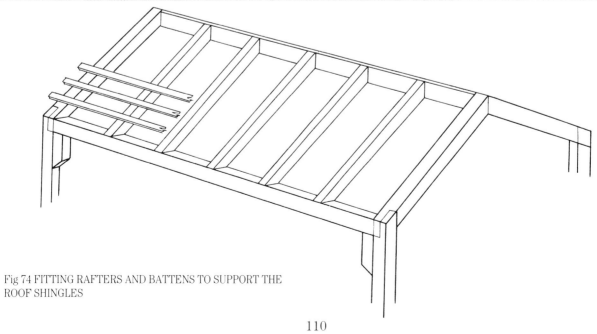

Fig 74 FITTING RAFTERS AND BATTENS TO SUPPORT THE
ROOF SHINGLES

ROOF · Cut two blocks ¼ x ⁷⁄₃₂ x ¾in long and glue in place to the top of the front uprights (see Fig 69A) to support the front top cross piece. Cut the front top cross piece and glue in place across the supports. Cut a second cross piece and glue in place at the bottom front edge. Cut the ridge beam from ¹⁄₁₆in wood-strip and glue into the notches in the side apexes. Cut ten rafters from ¹⁄₈ x ⁷⁄₃₂in wood to butt between the ridge beam and top cross pieces (five to each side of the roof). Space the rafters evenly and glue in place. Allow to dry thoroughly (Fig 74).

PLANKING · The four outside corners of the shed are edged with upright posts which extend from the ground to the roof-line and are cut from ³⁄₃₂ x ⁷⁄₃₂in wood. The

Plate 20 CONTENTS OF THE POTTING SHED

planks are butted together horizontally and fit inside this framework of upright posts.

Cut four corner posts and glue them to the back and front of the shed so that half the width of each post overhangs by ³⁄₃₂in (see Fig 75). The top edges are angled to follow the roof-line. Each plank has its top edge chamfered inside and outside, to make a good definition between the planks (Fig 75a). Cut, chamfer, fit and glue the planks, one at a time, working from the bottom upwards. The planking looks more realistic if, in some places, shorter lengths are fitted together to make up a plank. Glue each plank inside the corner posts and to the framework. Planks will need to be trimmed to fit around

111

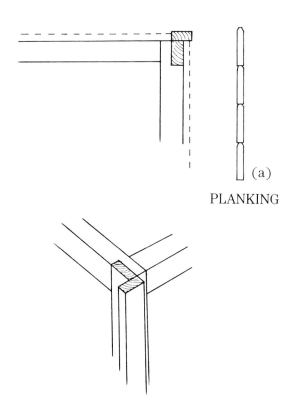

(a)

PLANKING

Fig 75 THE OUTSIDE CORNER POSTS FITTED TO ACCOMMODATE THE PLANKING

the door and window and shaped at the ends to fit into the side apexes. Finish the top of the side walls with barge-boarding cut from 1/16 x 3/16in wood-strip, mitred at the apex and glued to the planking.

ROOF SHINGLES · The wooden shingles are hung on battens. Cut battens in 1/8 x 1/64in fine wood-strip to over-hang the barge-boarding by 3/16in at each side. Cut twelve battens, six for each side of the roof. Glue the first batten (on each side) across the rafters at the front edge of the roof, and subsequent battens spaced at 5/8in intervals (Fig 74). Allow to dry. Start hanging the shingles from the roof edge and work upwards. Trim the first row of shing-les to 3/4in long and glue to the first batten, to overhang the top cross pieces by 1/4in. Trim subsequent rows of shingles to 1 1/8in long and glue to the remaining battens, each row overlapping and glued to the previous one so that 5/8in of shingle is exposed. Hang the shingles so that the joins alternate on each row, and trim the top rows so that they meet at the apex. Sand the shingles with rough sandpaper to remove any sharp edges. The apex is finished with a strip of lead folded along the centre and glued in place with UHU. A strip of fine sandpaper, painted to represent roofing felt, might be used as an alternative. This lead strip is approximately 1/2in wide.

DOORSILL · A small doorsill, cut from scrap timber and carved to look worn, is glued to the outside, beneath the door.

OUTSIDE

PAINTING · The inside of the shed was left as natural wood, but the outside was painted to represent a weathered effect. Use a piece of weathered wood – from a fence, shed or similar – as a guide for colour. Poster or acrylic paints can be used, mixed fairly watery so that the colour sinks into the wood and the grain and texture of the wood are still visible.

Put blobs of paint onto a dinner plate in shades of dark grey, light grey, dark brown, black and moss green. Mix colours and paint the shed all over as an undercoat. When this is dry, mix colours and paint the roof shingles and the planks individually, making slight variations in colour between one shingle and the next and one plank and the next. You might find it helpful to study a life-size wooden shed to see how weathering affects the colour of the wood. Define the edges of the planks and the roof shing-les with a watery wash of moss green mixed with a little black. Leave the paint to dry thoroughly.

THE BASE · The shed stands on a 3/8in thick plywood base, 18 x 10in, to allow space for some garden around the potting shed.

Cut the plywood and sand both sides and all the edges thoroughly. Stand the shed on the base in the position you want and trace around it with a sharp pencil. Lay out the garden effect you want and glue it to the base. We made a brick path along one side of the shed with an area of brick on the other side for the mangle to stand on. The remainder of the base is papered with good-quality flocked grass-effect paper. For full instructions on making brick and grass, etc, see pp75 and 80. Glue the bottom of the potting shed to the base. Edge the plywood base with 3/8 x 1/8in wood-strip that has been stained with walnut wood-stain and with mitred corners and glued in place with im-pact adhesive. Add plants and accessories as required, gluing them in place. We made a small flower-bed (see Chapter 6) at the back of the shed and a clump of flowers by the door. A pile of logs with sawdust – cut from small branches – is glued to the base at the back. The clumps of moss in the path are small pieces of chenille knitting yarn, glued in place and dabbed with moss green paint. The mud is tea, from a teabag, blown into glue squeezed into the cracks between the bricks.

MANGLE · The mangle is made of white metal, from a kit from Phoenix Model Developments (see list of stockists, p176) who make a wide range of white metal kits for items ranging from fireplaces to sewing-machines. The mangle was painted with matt black and dark grey Humbrol enamel paint to represent a weathered effect, while the wooden rollers are left in their natural colour.

WHITE METAL KITS · If you are using a white metal kit for the first time, check with the parts list that you have all the pieces necessary to make the model. Look at the pieces critically and check that they are not distorted and that the detail is well defined. Most white metal castings are made in vulcanised rubber moulds which have a limited life and which when past their best produce distorted castings. If any of your pieces are distorted, return the kit for an exchange. The white metal pieces will probably have small areas of excess, flaky metal (flashing) at seam lines and edges. These should be removed with a craft knife. You may also find mould lines – a slight ridge where the two halves of the mould are joined – and these should be smoothed with either a fine needle file or a craft knife. When the pieces are clean, read the assembly instructions from beginning to end and be sure that you understand them. Dry-fit the pieces together at each stage before assembling them with glue. If necessary, trim with the craft knife or needle file. Assemble the kit with a fast-drying epoxy resin adhesive, following the instructions and allowing each stage to dry thoroughly before proceeding to the next. Never exert excessive pressure on any part during assembly as the metal is very soft and will bend or distort easily. It is often easier to paint tiny or inaccessible parts of a kit before you assemble it.

White metal is best painted with enamel or acrylic paint. If you use acrylic, the paint will need to be sealed with varnish. Paint the model with a coat of matt white primer, allow this to dry thoroughly, then paint the base colour. When this is dry, paint the detail. Use very fine, good-quality brushes to paint fine details. Consider 'customising' white metal kits, for example the white metal base of a sewing-machine might be removed and replaced with a wooden one.

INSIDE

RUSH MAT · On the floor of the potting shed is a rush mat made from a table-mat (or beach mat) of thin rush strips, stitched together. When cut, the rushes fall apart, so cut a much larger piece than you need, gently pull out the excess rushes and knot the threads which hold them together in pairs. This will prevent further rushes from pulling out. Dirty the mat with a wet teabag or paint and sprinkle a little mud (tea) over the floor.

DECKCHAIR · The deckchair is made of $\frac{1}{8}$ x $\frac{1}{12}$in hardwood – beech or ramin is ideal – and you will need approximately 30in. The deckchair is made up of three frames; the smallest fits inside the second and the second inside the third (Fig 76). It is essential that measuring and cutting are done accurately to ensure that these three pieces fit together. To make the smallest frame, cut two sides and drill $\frac{1}{16}$in diameter holes at each end to receive the rails. Mark and cut the notches on both sides – this is best done by cutting a shallow 'V' with a craft knife and hollowing it into a notch with a round needle file. Cut two rails that are sufficiently long to whittle pegs at each end. Fit and glue the rails into the sides, ensuring that the

piece is square and lies perfectly flat on the work surface. When the frame is dry, use a needle file and fine abrasive paper to round off all the edges.

The middle frame is constructed in exactly the same way, except that the sides are not notched, and the largest frame is also constructed in the same way, except that it has only one rail.

To assemble the deckchair, drill holes through the sides of each frame at points A and B as shown on the pattern. The pieces are pinned together with fine brass pins so the drilled holes should tightly fit the diameter of the pins you use. Place the smaller frame inside the middle frame, lining up points A. Insert pins from the outside through both pieces, mark the pins for trimming and remove. Trim the pins to length, squeeze a little Superglue into the holes in the smaller frame, and push the pins into place. If necessary, smooth down the ends of the pins with a fine needle file until they are flush with the frame. Fit and pin the larger frame at points B to glued holes in the middle frame.

Locate the back rail in the notches. Cut a piece of cotton fabric, $4\frac{1}{4}$ x $1\frac{1}{2}$in. Seal the edges with Fraycheck or glue. Fold one short end and glue over the top rail, and fold and glue the other short end over the seat rail.

STEP-LADDER · The ladder should be made in hardwood, such as beech or ramin. Cut and assemble the front and back separately (Fig 77). For the front, cut two sides and mark the position of each step. Cut grooves on these marks with a craft knife, metal rule and watchmaker's 'chisel' to receive the steps. Cut six steps, taking measurements carefully from the pattern. Glue the top and bottom steps into the grooves in the sides, place the assembly on the pattern to check that it is square and leave to dry. Glue the remaining steps into place. Cut the top back piece (A), note that the top edge is cut to the same angle as the sides and glue in place.

For the back, cut two sides as shown on the pattern, noting that the top and bottom edges are slightly angled. Cut the top back-piece (B), the two cross braces and one diagonal brace. Note that (B) fits between the sides and the braces are butted onto the sides. Glue and assemble the sides, top back-piece and braces, using the pattern to check that the assembly is square and lies flat on the work surface.

Place the back and front together so that pieces A and B line up and mark the placement for the hinges. (Note that the hinges must fit vertically, and not follow the taper of the ladder.) Cut recesses to receive the hinges and glue them into place with Superglue.

Cut the top and glue in place. Drill $\frac{1}{16}$in diameter holes through the centre of the bottom step and the bottom brace and thread fine string knotted at both ends.

The ladder is painted to look old and used, using a mixture of green, brown and grey paint which was allowed to dry, then spattered with magnolia paint. To spatter, simply load the brush with paint and flick this onto the ladder from a distance of approximately 12in.

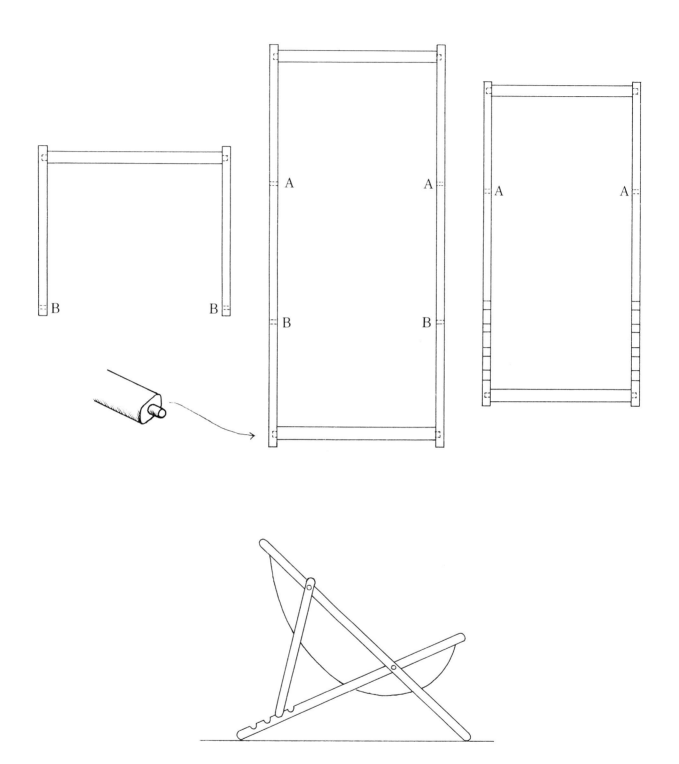

Fig 76 PATTERN FOR THE DECKCHAIR

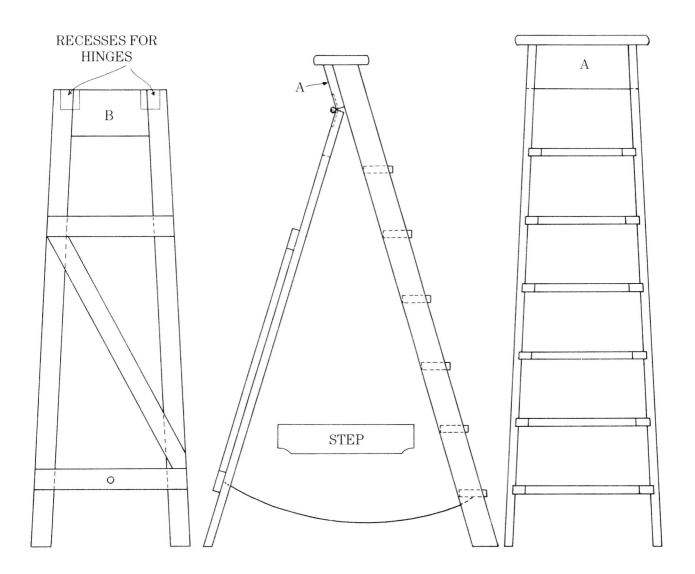

RECESSES FOR
HINGES

B

A

A

STEP

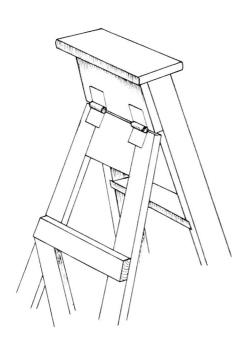

Fig 77 PATTERN AND ASSEMBLY FOR THE LADDER

BOXES · The boxes are the same as those made for Russel Sprout in Chapter 4, p57. They are 'dirtied' with greeny brown paint. To make a box of seedlings, mix tea and white glue to make 'mud'. Spread this in the box and prick holes as it dries with a wooden toothpick. Cut snippets of green leafy material and glue them into the pricked holes. Fill another box with kindling, cut from twigs, and another with old newspapers, cut from magazines and newspaper pages, tied in bundles with button thread. If the newspapers look too clean, wipe a damp teabag over them to make them yellowed and dirty.

BROOM · Cut a small handful of bristles from a life-size broom and cut a 4in length of thin dowelling or use a straight twig for the handle. Bundle the bristles and trim them all to the same length at the top. Hold them firmly in one hand, push the handle down into the centre of the bundle and bind tightly with button thread. Trim the bristle ends roughly to length.

HOSE · Use any suitable green plastic tube or, if this is not available, paint a length of string or cord (or similar) green. (The hose must coil neatly so check this before selecting the material.) The nozzles are cut down from the nozzles supplied with tins of cigarette lighter fuel and glued to each end of the hose. Any similar oddments might be used.

ACCESSORIES · The compost is real potting compost (or tea) in small plastic bags with labels cut from magazine advertisements.

The packets of weed-killer, slug repellent etc are small pieces of wood, lengths of dowelling or plastic oddments. The packets are wrapped in paper and the labels are cut from gardening magazine advertisements or catalogues for gardening products.

Small bundles of raffia and button thread 'string' hang from nails and a small checked rag is soaked in water to make it hang in realistic folds. The beer bottle is another plastic nozzle painted dark brown with an advertisement cut-out label. Seed packets, calendar and pin-up are all magazine cut-outs. The miniature gardening magazines have typing-paper pages stapled into covers cut from advertisements for 'next month's issue'.

BOUGHT ITEMS · The other contents of the potting shed are fine quality miniatures from specialist craftsmen. The potted plants are from Carolyn Smith and the vegetables from Rohanna Bryan. The paint tin and saw are from Dolphin Miniatures. The spade and fork, shears, trowel and fork are from Quality Dolls' House Miniatures. The tools are muddied with a little brown paint. The muddy boots and the chopping-block are from Mini Mansions (see list of stockists, pp176–8).

9

THE ATTIC

The attic is a more demanding project for the builder with some experience. It represents a small attic room in a Tudor house and is designed to be architecturally convincing. The building is made of plywood, with applied timbering. The roof is tiled with self-hardening clay and the dormer window has leaded lights. Inside, the room is partitioned to provide a small landing which, in the imagination, leads to a staircase. The attic may be furnished as a cottage bedroom if you prefer, but it has been used here to display a small collection of fine-quality craftsman-made miniatures.

This chapter includes full instructions for making the building. Furniture patterns can be found in Chapters 2, 5, 10 and 11 if you wish to furnish the attic as a room, and full details of the items in our attic are given below. This chapter also includes instructions for modelling dolls.

Fig 78 PATTERN FOR THE ATTIC WALLS

TO MAKE THE ATTIC

You will find it helpful to refer to Chapter 1 for notes on construction and assembling doors and windows.

For the main construction of the attic, use ⅜in plywood for the walls and floor; the roof is assembled separately.

Cut two gabled sides, one floor and one back wall as shown in Fig 78. Cut notches in the tops of the gable walls as shown, to receive the ridge pole. Glue and pin the back wall onto the floor. Glue and pin the gable walls to the outside of the floor and back wall. The top edge of the back wall must be faced at this stage with 'timbering' to simulate a beam.

The timbering is made from a suitable hardwood stained as required before fitting; we have used elm coloured with walnut wood stain. To face the top edge of the back wall, cut a ⅜ x ⅛in strip of timbering, stain and glue in place. When this facing is in place, the top of the

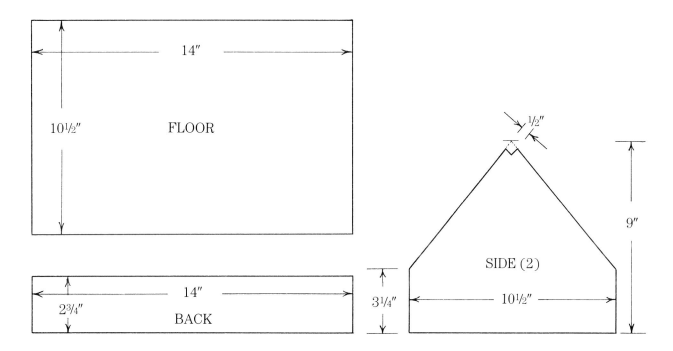

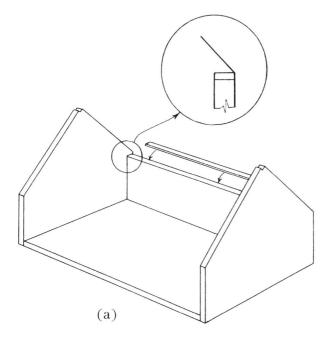

(a)

Fig 78a: ASSEMBLY OF THE ATTIC WALLS

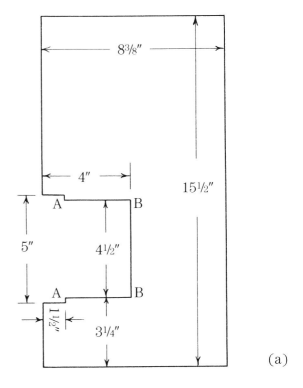

(a)

back wall lines up with the angle of the gable walls (Fig 78a).

The ridge pole is made from ½in square section wood, cut to fit into the notches in the top of the gable walls. Plane the top faces of the ridge pole so that the angles of these faces follow the angles of the gable walls. Do not glue the ridge pole in place at this stage.

BACK ROOF · The back of the roof and the dormer window are constructed together. The roof is made of ⅛in plywood; the dormer is made of ¼in plywood roofed with ¹⁄₁₆in plywood with a ceiling of ⅛in plywood.

Cut the back roof as shown in Fig 79a, including the cut-out for the dormer. Note that the edges (A) and (B) of the dormer cut-out are chamfered to follow the lines of the dormer pieces (see Fig 79b).

Glue and pin the ridge pole to the top edge of the back roof so that the roof overhangs the ridge pole equally at each side. To hold the back roof temporarily in place while the dormer window is assembled, fit the ridge pole into the notches on the gable walls and tap a pin lightly through the lower edge of the roof into the back wall at each side.

Cut the dormer front and sides in ¼in plywood (Fig 80). Glue and pin the sides behind the front so that the top edges of the sides meet the angles of the front (Fig 81a). Dry-fit the assembly in place and make any minor adjustments necessary to ensure that the back wall and dormer are flush and that the bottom edge of the dormer rests squarely on the top edge of the back wall. When a good fit is achieved, glue the dormer sides onto the roof (Fig 81b).

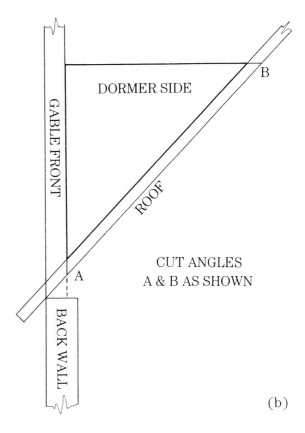

(b)

Fig 79 (A) PATTERN FOR BACK ROOF; (B) POSITION OF DORMER SIDE ON THE ROOF

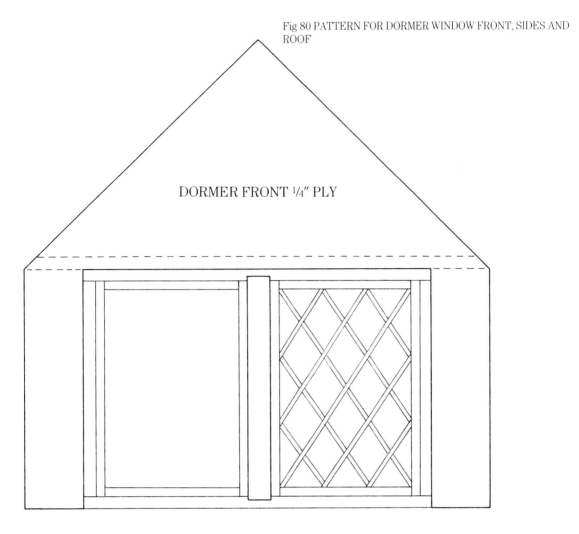

Fig 80 PATTERN FOR DORMER WINDOW FRONT, SIDES AND ROOF

DORMER FRONT ¼″ PLY

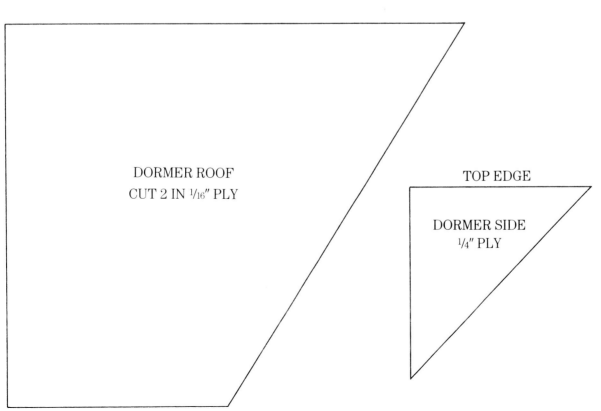

DORMER ROOF
CUT 2 IN ¹⁄₁₆″ PLY

TOP EDGE

DORMER SIDE
¼″ PLY

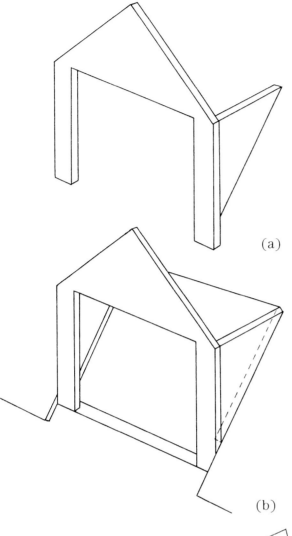

(a)

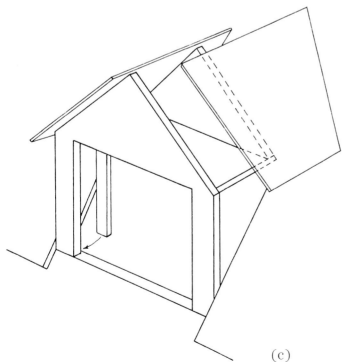

(b)

Cut the dormer ceiling from ⅛in plywood and glue it in place across the top of the dormer sides. Note that the side edges of the ceiling are chamfered to the same angle as the dormer front.

Cut a triangular support for the back of the dormer roof in ¼in plywood. Simply use the triangular part of the dormer front as a pattern. Glue the support onto the back edge of the dormer ceiling (see Fig 81c).

To cut the dormer roof pieces, use the pattern in Fig 80 to cut templates in thin cardboard. Fit and adjust the templates as necessary so that the angles are a perfect fit, then use the templates to cut the roof pieces in ¹⁄₁₆in plywood. Glue the dormer roof pieces onto the dormer front and back support. Tape the join at the roof apex with masking-tape.

WINDOW · To make the window you will need Lexan sheet (or similar thin perspex) and lead strip, which is sold for making stained-glass projects. The window is framed with stained wood-strip – either commercial wood-strip or cut from hardwood. Face the inner sides of the window frame with ⅛in thick wood to build up to the same thickness as the back wall (see Fig 81c). Build a frame of ⅛in thick wood into the window opening. Note that the top and bottom of this frame have grooves cut to receive the mullion. Cut the mullion, ¼in wide, in ⅜in thick wood, and glue it in place (Fig 82). Frame both window openings with ³⁄₂in square wood-strip. Fit these frames ¹⁄₁₆in from the inside edge of the window openings and glue in place (see Fig 3, p11). Cut windows in thin perpex to fit

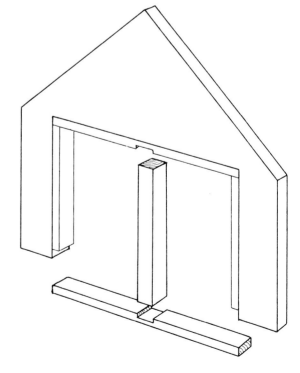

(c)

Fig 81 STAGES IN DORMER-WINDOW CONSTRUCTION

Fig 82 FRAMING THE WINDOW AND FITTING THE MULLION

against the frames and glue in place with a little UHU or similar glue. Fit a second frame of ³/₂in square wood-strip behind the perspex and glue in place.

To make the leaded lights, use lead strip backed with double-sided Sellotape, which is simpler and neater than glue. Cut a 3in length of lead strip and smooth it out as flat and as even as possible. Stick one side of the tape firmly to the lead strip (leaving the tape backing in place). With a craft knife and metal ruler, cut the taped lead into fine strips. Using a tracing of the pattern (see Fig 80) tacked to the inside of the window as a guide, peel off the tape backing and position the lead strips in one diagonal direction, trimming each strip to fit. Press these firmly in place, then fit the strips in the other diagonal direction. Use your thumb-nail to crease the lead where the strips cross and trim the ends to fit.

As the back roof is only held in place temporarily, it may be removed and replaced as you wish, while the window is built, glazed and leaded. Remove the roof to make easier access while you plank the floor.

FLOOR · The floor is planked with pre-glued iron-on veneer – we have used oak (available from DIY shops). Cut the veneer into ⁵/₈in wide strips. The strips are laid at random to avoid matching the grain and cut to differing lengths to simulate joins in the planks. The colour plates show how they are laid, with a fractional gap between each plank. Start at the back of the room and work forward, using an iron set to medium heat to fix one plank at a time. As the glue melts, use a wooden block to press each plank down firmly. If necessary, iron the finished floor again to ensure that all the planks are thoroughly bonded. Mark the 'nail heads' in pencil.

CHIMNEY-BREAST · Replace the back roof, temporarily, while you make the chimney-breast. The chimney-breast is cut from a block of 1in thick balsa wood, faced with ¹/₈in plywood. Cut the balsa and plywood from the pattern (Fig 83) and glue together, clamping until thoroughly dry. The wooden fireplace surround is cut from ¹/₈in thick pine (or similar) and the central arched piece from black cardboard. The mantelshelf is a piece of cornice moulding. To make the surround, cut two sides and one lintel from the pattern, stain and polish as required and glue them to the chimney-breast so that half the width of each piece overhangs the fireplace opening. Cut the cardboard piece and glue it behind the overhanging area of the surround. Cut and glue the mantelshelf to rest above the lintel. Paint the insides of the fireplace opening and the area of the side wall where the fireplace will fit with matt black paint. Cut a hearth in black paper and glue it to the underside of the chimney-breast and fireplace. Glue the back of the chimney breast and the underside of the hearth and fit in place, so that the angle at the top of the chimney-breast butts against the underside of the back roof.

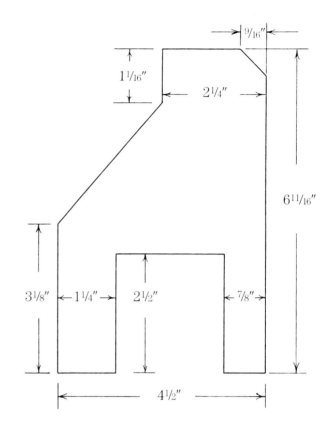

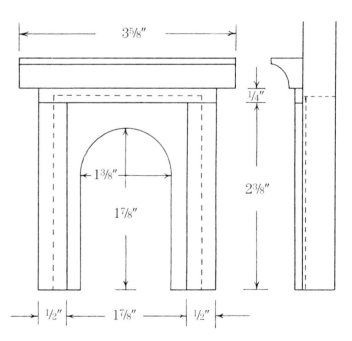

Fig 83 PATTERN FOR CHIMNEY-BREAST AND FIREPLACE

Plate 21 'MEMORIES':
THE ATTIC

THE ATTIC

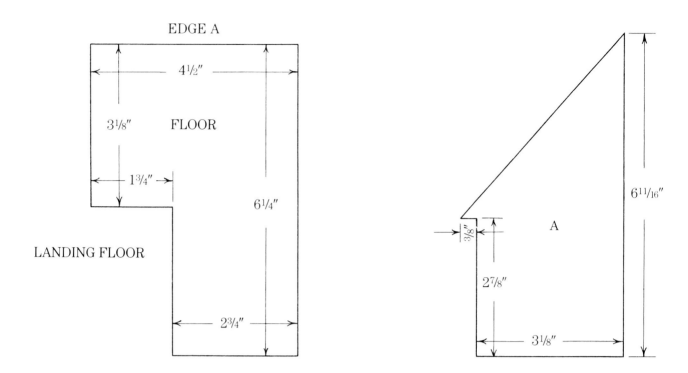

EDGE A

4½″

3⅛″   FLOOR

1¾″

6¼″

LANDING FLOOR

2¾″

A

6¹¹/₁₆″

3/8″

2⅞″

3⅛″

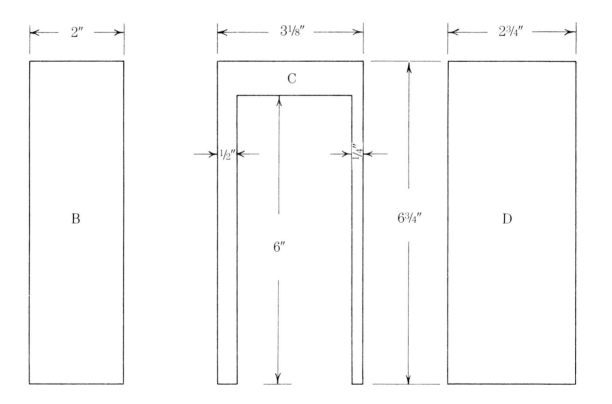

2″

B

3⅛″

C

½″   ¼″

6″

6¾″

2¾″

D

Fig 84 PATTERNS FOR LANDING FLOOR AND WALLS

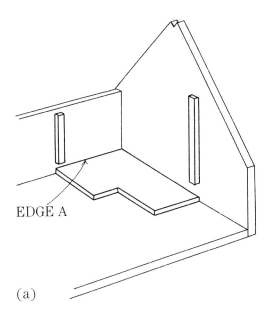

EDGE A

(a)

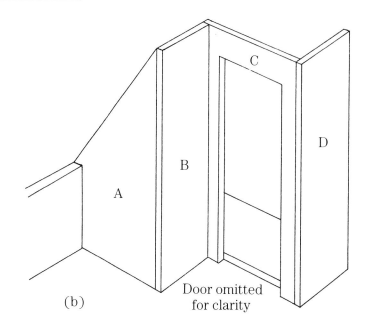

C

B

A

D

Door omitted
for clarity

(b)

PARTITION WALL · The partition wall is built around a raised floor on the 'landing' behind the partition. Cut the landing floor from the pattern (Fig 84) in ¼in thick plywood. Plank the floor with iron-on veneer and glue it in place (Fig 85a) so that edge (A) rests along the back wall. Cut two support strips of ⅜ x ¼in wood and glue them to the back and side walls to line up with the edges of the 'landing' floor as shown in the diagram. Use a set square to check that these support strips are perfectly vertical. Cut the partition wall pieces from the pattern in Fig 84 in ¼in thick plywood.

Note that the door is made and hinged in place before the partition walls are fitted. Whilst working on partition wall (C) (Fig 85), build the door-frame from ¹⁄₁₆in wood-strip, which should be stained before fitting.

DOOR · Make the door from ³⁄₃₂in thick wood (stained as required) to fit the door-frame; it may be assembled from ½in planks, butted together or one piece of wood scored to resemble planks. Cut cross braces in ½in x ³⁄₃₂in wood and glue to the landing side of the door. Note that the cross braces fit flush with the edge of the door on the hinged side, but should end ³⁄₃₂in short on the other edge to ensure that the door will close over the door-frame. Cut recesses to receive the hinges in the door and door-frame and fix the hinges in place with Superglue. Commercial brass door-handles, painted with matt black enamel paint and fixed with Superglue, have been used. Cut and fit a simple architrave of ³⁄₃₂ x ⅛in wood-strip to frame the door on the room side.

Now you can assemble the partition walls, A, B, C and D, one at a time (Fig 85b). Glue D to the outside edge of the landing floor and to the support strip and the side wall. Glue C (with the door) to the landing floor and wall D. Glue A to the landing floor and the support strip and the back wall. (Check that the angled edge of A butts against the underside of the back roof.) Glue B to the

Fig 85 ASSEMBLY OF LANDING FLOOR AND WALLS

landing floor and the edges of walls A and C. Cut a small strip of ¹⁄₁₆in thick wood to fit the edge of the landing floor in the doorway. Try it in place to check that the door closes; trim if necessary and glue in place.

At this stage, the back roof is still not fixed, so there is access from above to decorate the landing.

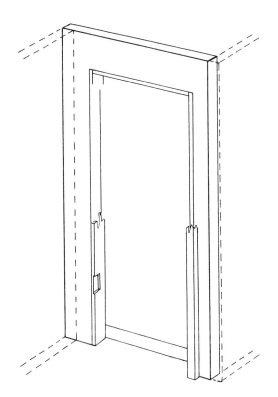

Fig 86 MAKING THE DOOR-FRAME

Plate 22 THE ATTIC – UNFURNISHED

DECORATING

INTERIOR · Paint is applied before the beams are fitted and wallpaper is applied after the beams are fitted. Paint the walls and underside of the back roof with two or three coats of matt-finish emulsion paint (we used magnolia and 'aged' the finish with patches of coffee paint, blended in while the magnolia was wet).

The beams are made from strips of ³⁄₃₂in thick hardwood (we used elm). To give a rough and irregular effect, cut the beams with a fret-saw with deliberately uneven edges. Use a drum sander with a coarse abrasive in the drill and shape an uneven surface on one side of the beam. The drum sander will produce a rough finish, which resembles hewn beams. Stain the beams and allow to dry, then sand lightly with rough sandpaper to heighten the colour effect of old beams. Using the colour plate as a guide for positioning the beams, cut and glue them in place to the walls (including the landing). You may find it easier to cut the curved brace beams by first making a cardboard template. Note that the back roof (and ceiling) are beamed later, when the roof is fitted in place. Cut, fit and paste wallpaper between the beams.

The back roof is now fixed in place by gluing and pinning along the gable walls.

CEILING · Cut a ceiling from ⅛in thick plywood to rest across the top of the chimney-breast and partition walls. Chamfer the back to fit flush against the back roof and the front edge to the same angle as the gable walls. Paint the ceiling and glue in place to the chimney-breast, partition walls and the back roof (Fig 87). Cut and fit beams to the ceiling and back roof.

Cut the front roof from ⅛in plywood, to meet the back roof at the ridge pole and the bottom of the ceiling at the front edge. Glue and pin the front roof to the gable walls and the ridge pole.

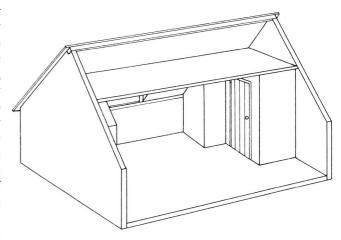

Fig 87 FITTING THE CEILING IN PLACE

EXTERIOR · Paint the exterior walls with two or three coats of matt emulsion paint (we used magnolia, 'aged' with coffee paint). Use the colour plate as a guide to cut and fit the beams. When the beams are fixed, apply another coat of paint to the walls, working right up to the edges of the beams to minimise the 'stuck on' effect.

CHIMNEY · The chimney is made of 1in thick balsa wood, covered with self-hardening clay (we used terracotta Das). Cut the balsa block from the pattern (Fig 88). Roll out the clay to ⅛in thickness and allow to dry. (An 8in square area of rolled-out clay will be more than enough for the chimney.) When the clay sheet is dry, cut (with a craft knife and metal rule) and glue with UHU to the four sides of the chimney. Cut and fit a second layer of clay around the top edge of the chimney (see Fig 88). Fill any cracks or gaps with a little wet clay rubbed in with the finger. Mark the bricks on the clay in pencil and cut shallow grooves between the bricks with a craft knife. Define the bricks with a watchmaker's screwdriver or similar tool.

Turn in wood (or model in clay) two chimney-pots and set them into a fillet of wet clay on top of the chimney. Glue the chimney to the roof, following the line of the chimney-breast.

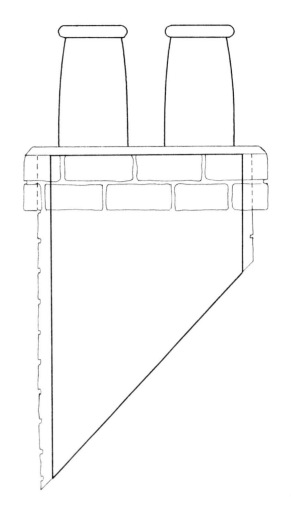

Fig 88 PATTERN FOR CHIMNEY

TILES · The roof tiles are made of self-hardening clay – we used terracotta Das. You will need two packets of clay to make the roof-tiles and bricks for the chimney. Roll out the clay as thin as possible – ideally ¹⁄₁₆in thick – and allow the clay sheets to dry. Cut the clay into 1in wide strips. Sand the strips with medium-grade sandpaper to make the top edge as thin as possible and tapered so that the tile strips have a wedge-shaped profile. Mark the strips into ⅝in wide tiles with pencil. Score the marks with a craft knife to define individual tiles. With the craft knife, work along each strip of tiles, cut back one or two lower edges, chip off a small corner or pare edges and sides, so that the tiles look irregular rather than uniform (Fig 89). Starting at the lower edge and working up to the ridge, glue the tile strips to the roof with UHU or similar glue. Glue each row of tiles so that they overlap the previous row, leaving approximately ½in of tile exposed. Tile the main roof first, trimming the tiles to fit around the dormer roof; then tile the dormer roof, lining the tiles up with those on the main roof and trimming the tiles as necessary to fit. Use wet clay, applied to dampened roof tiles to make a fillet around the chimney-stack, pressing it firmly in place with the finger (see Plate 23, p130). The ridges on the main roof and the dormer are made of clay strips, formed over a square edge until dry, then scored into individual tiles approximately 1¼in long and glued in place. When the ridges are in place, use the craft knife to pare dips and hollows in some tiles along the top edge so that the ridge is not uniform.

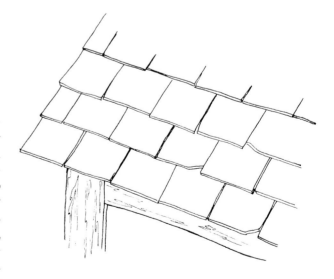

Fig 89 ROOF TILES

The roof tiles and the chimney are painted with poster or acrylic paints. Put blobs of paint – dark brown, grey, light brown, scarlet, yellow ochre, olive green and black –

onto a dinner plate. Mix grey, olive green and black, and paint the mortar between the bricks on the chimney and the fillets around and on top of the chimney. Use mixes of brown, scarlet and yellow ochre to paint the bricks, painting each brick individually. Paint the roof tiles with mixes of the colours on the plate, using greeny-black to give a weathered effect to areas along the ridges and where the dormer joins the main roof. The paint should be used fairly thickly so that it does not 'disappear' into the bricks and tiles, and it is worth studying tiled roofs and chimneys to check the colours. Paint the chimney-pots – terracotta on the outside, black on the inside.

The attic is finished by facing the raw edges of the plywood with timbering. Use the drum sander to blend the edges of this facing into the timbers on the outside of the gable wall so that the finished effect looks like a solid beam. Use the same technique to blend the corners where side and back walls meet.

CONTENTS · The attic has been filled with a variety of items. They are all good quality commercial miniatures (see list of stockists, pp175–9.) The tapestry armchair and the cane and wood rocking-cradle are from Dijon Importers; the patchwork quilt in the cradle is from The Dolls' House. The violin and case are from The Singing Tree and the cane birdcage is from Mini Mansions. The cabin trunk, from The Mulberry Bush, has a lift-out tray which has been filled with tiny photographs, ribbon-tied documents and letters written with a fine point (Rotring) drawing-pen. The rolled carpet is made from a needlepoint kit from Jean Brown and the stained-glass panel and lampshade are from Wentways Miniatures. The splendid rocking-horse and the model ship in a case are both from Dolphin Miniatures. The wooden sewing-machine case belongs to the machine in the 'Dollmaker's Workroom'. Isobel Hockey knitted the tiny dress and the old lady's shawl. Instructions for the tailors' dummy can be found on pp87–8. Other items are from the author's collection.

MAKING MODELLED DOLLS

The simplest rag dolls in Chapter 2 are quite at home in their shoebox settings, but more sophisticated projects require more realistic dolls. Several of the specialist suppliers sell dolls, ranging from characters like Russel Sprout in Chapter 4 to the elegant Edwardian lady in Chapter 10, or you may prefer to buy a porcelain doll-kit and make the body and clothes yourself. Although the range of commercial dolls and kits is wide, and the quality generally very good, you may prefer to make your own. The method described here, though obviously not the only one, is the one we use. The heads and limbs of the dolls are modelled in self-hardening or oven-fired clay onto a skeleton of pipecleaners. Of the clays available, we recommend 'Fimo', which is hardened in a domestic oven and is available from art and craft shops, or 'La Doll'

which air-dries and is available from Recollect (see list of stockists, p176).

Fimo is available in small packets and you will need one packet of flesh colour and one packet of white as the colour sold as 'flesh' is too dark. The clay is kneaded thoroughly to soften it before use, and the flesh and white must be kneaded together to produce a realistic flesh tone. The texture is rather like Plasticine – it will take finely modelled detail and the finished surface is smooth. Although the kneading is tiresome as the two colours must be thoroughly mixed, it is very easy to work with and is probably the best choice for the beginner as it needs only to be hardened before the detail is painted in. La Doll has a finer texture than any other air-hardening clay we have used. It works very like ordinary clay and dries to an off-white finish which is smoothed with very fine abrasive paper and painted with Humbrol enamel paints, mixing matt white and flesh colours together to make a pale flesh tone resembling porcelain. Whichever material you choose, the method is the same.

Fig 90 shows the finished proportions of adult and child-size dolls. Keep this figure in front of you as you work to check that you are making the doll parts the right size. To make the head, roll a ball of clay approximately 1in in diameter. Fold a pipecleaner in half and push the ends well into the clay ball. The tools you use to model the head are a matter of personal preference. We find that much of the work is done with the fingers, with a wooden toothpick and fine paint-brush to make small details. Experiment and use whatever you find most useful. Hold the pipecleaner 'stalk' while you mould and model the head to shape. Build up the forehead, chin and nose and define the eyes and mouth. If you are a beginner, don't worry about detail; get the basic shape of the head right and get a suggestion of the nose. More detail will come with experience, but even simple modelling will make effective dolls. Eyes, eyebrows and mouth will be painted in later, and moustaches and wrinkles may also be painted on rather than modelled. Check the head constantly from all angles to make sure that it has a good profile and both sides are symmetrical. When you have a good shape, smooth the head as thoroughly as possible. If you have used Fimo, use your fingers and a slightly dampened cotton bud; if you have used La Doll, use a small paint-brush and water. Knead a little clay between your fingers to flatten it and wrap this around the pipecleaner below the head to make the neck. Blend the clay up under the chin and the back of the head. Leave the head standing in a small cup or jar while you make the limbs.

Only the lower part of the limbs is modelled – the legs and feet to just below the knee and the arms and hands to just below the elbow. Model each limb onto a separate pipecleaner. Wrap the clay around the pipecleaner to make a 'sausage' with the pipecleaner in the centre. For the arms, press the clay between the fingers to flatten it to shape the hands, squeeze and roll to narrow the wrists and plump out for the lower arm. Define the fingers with the toothpick and, if you wish, separate the thumb, cut-

Fig 90 DOLL PROPORTIONS

ting through the clay with a craft knife. Check the length – the lower arm must not be too long, or the arm will not bend naturally at the elbow. Gently position the hands as you want them and stand the arms in the jar with the head. For the legs, wrap a clay sausage around the pipe-cleaner and bend the foot forward. Flatten the feet by pressing them between your fingers, roll and squeeze to shape the ankle and plump out the calf. Check the length – the legs should bend naturally at the knee, so the lower leg must not be too long. Unless you wish, there is no need to define the toes as the feet will be covered by shoes, or you may prefer to model (and paint) shoes or boots on the feet. Place the feet together sole to sole to check that they are the same size and make sure you have made a pair of hands and a pair of feet. The modelled parts can all stand in the jar to air-dry or to be hardened in the oven.

When dry, Fimo parts will be ready to paint in the detail. La Doll parts should be sanded smooth, very gently with fine grade abrasive paper and finished by rubbing all over with a piece of nylon stocking. When the parts are smooth, paint on two coats of Humbrol matt enamel, allowing the first coat to dry thoroughly before the second is applied. (Stand the parts in the jar while the paint dries.) If your doll is going to wear a dress with a low neckline, she will need modelled shoulders and chest. In this case, assemble the doll, then build the chest and shoulders in clay over the body and reharden in the oven or leave to dry. (La Doll should be painted all together, after the added parts are dry.)

To assemble the doll, work with Fig 90 in front of you so that you can check the proportions. You will need ½in wide surgical tape and tubular gauze finger bandage – both available from chemist shops – and a little cotton wool for padding. Trim the doubled length of pipecleaner

Plate 23 THE ATTIC: BACK VIEW

which supports the head to the correct length – this makes the 'spine'. Trim both leg pipecleaners to fit alongside the 'spine', the top ends reaching to the doll's armpits. Tape around the legs and body to hold them together. Trim and bend the arm pipecleaners so that the bend forms the doll's shoulders and tape the arms securely to the body. Pad the upper arms and legs with wisps of cotton wool wrapped around the limbs and bind with surgical tape to hold the padding in place (Fig 91). Pad the body and hold the padding in place by pulling a length of tubular gauze finger bandage up over the cotton wool. Tuck in the raw edges and oversew the bandage together across the shoulders and under the crotch. To define the doll's waist, bind tightly with surgical tape. If the doll is to have modelled shoulders and bosom, roll the clay out to a thin sheet and lay this over the padded body. Shape the shoulders and bosom and smooth the clay into the lower edge of the neck. Harden the doll in the oven or leave to dry.

Paint the doll's features with poster or acrylic paints and very fine brushes. Use a little powder blusher on a cotton bud to colour the cheeks. Wigs may be made of embroidery silk or mohair or white animal wool (from chemist shops) for elderly dolls. Stitch the parting through the hair with tiny back stitches, coat the doll's head with UHU glue and carefully position the hair on the head. Wigs are usually better fitted after the doll is dressed.

Chapter 7 offers a selection of patterns for dressing lady dolls which may be adapted for men and children (see pp93, 96–7, 100–1). For example, for trousers, use the drawers pattern lengthened, and for shirts, use the bodice pattern reversed. Methods and making-up instructions are given with the patterns.

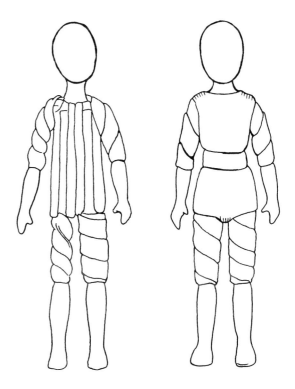

Fig 91 ASSEMBLING THE DOLL

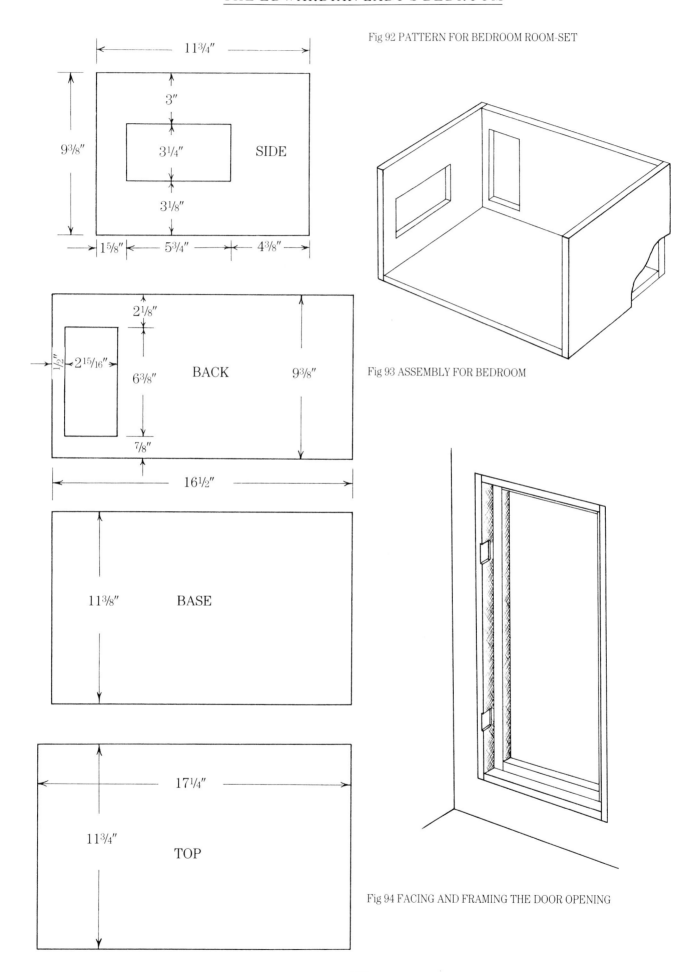

Fig 92 PATTERN FOR BEDROOM ROOM-SET

11¾"

9⅜"

3"

3¼"

SIDE

3⅛"

1⅝" 5¾" 4⅜"

2⅛"

½" 2¹⁵⁄₁₆"

BACK

6⅜"

9⅜"

7⅞"

16½"

11⅜" BASE

Fig 93 ASSEMBLY FOR BEDROOM

17¼"

11¾" TOP

Fig 94 FACING AND FRAMING THE DOOR OPENING

10
THE EDWARDIAN LADY'S BEDROOM

This project is designed for the more experienced furniture-maker though the room set is fairly simple to construct. It is made of ⅜in plywood and has a non-opening door and window and a corner chimney-breast. The furniture is made in pine, mahogany, yew and cherry, using authentic furniture-making methods. The full range of tools discussed in Chapter 1 has been used to make these pieces, though all joints may be cut by hand if you do not have a shaper table. Patterns and instructions are given here for the room set and the wooden furniture. The splendid brass bed is from The Dolls' House, and we have used a small bedroom fireplace from Sussex Crafts, although if you prefer to make the fireplace, instructions can be found in Chapters 2 and 9, pp27, 29 and 121. The Edwardian lady is a fine porcelain dressed doll from Sunday Dolls (see list of stockists, pp176–7 for details).

ROOM SET · Cut a base, a back and two sides from the pattern (Fig 92) in ⅜in plywood. Use a fret-saw to cut out the door opening in the back and the window opening in the left-hand side. Sand all surfaces and edges thoroughly. Glue and pin the back to the outside of the base. Glue and pin the sides to the outside of the base and to the back (Fig 93). The top is cut and fixed after the door, window and chimney-breast are fitted.

DOOR · The door is made from ⅛in thick wood, panelled with ¹⁄₁₆in thick wood. Face the edges of the door opening with ⅛in wood-strip, glued in place as shown in Fig 94. Note that the left-hand side should have recesses cut to accommodate the hinges. Do not fix the inner (second) frame at this stage as the frame is completed after the door is made.

Cut the door from ⅛in thick wood so that it fits into the frame, allowing a fractional gap all around. Cut the panelling in ¹⁄₁₆in thick wood from the pattern (Fig 95) and glue to the door (on one side of the door only). Sand the door thoroughly to reduce the thickness of the panelling by approximately one quarter. Cut recesses in the left-hand edge of the door to accommodate the hinges, corresponding with those in the door-frame.

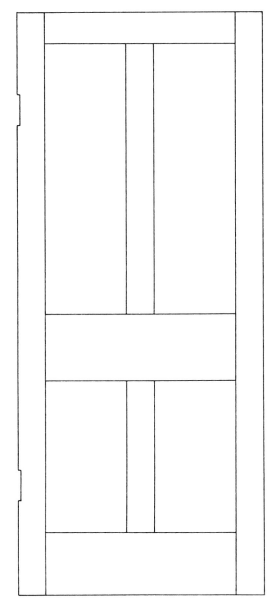

Fig 95 PATTERN FOR BEDROOM DOOR

Overleaf:
Plate 24 THE EDWARDIAN LADY'S BEDROOM

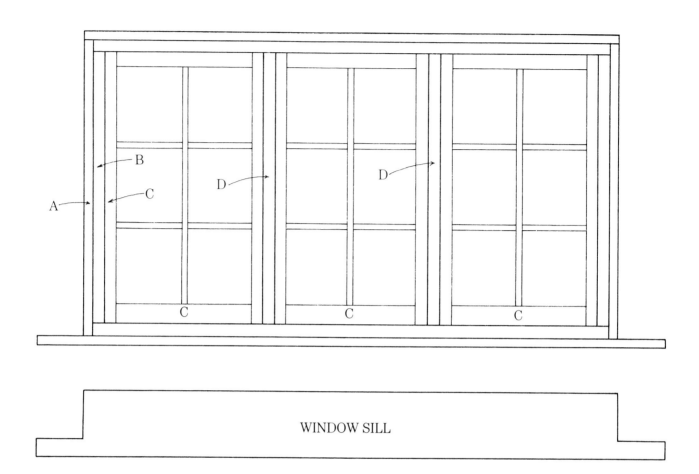

WINDOW SILL

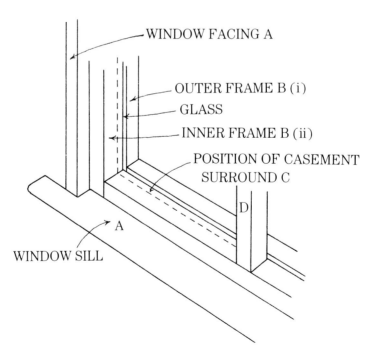

WINDOW FACING A

OUTER FRAME B (i)

GLASS

INNER FRAME B (ii)

POSITION OF CASEMENT
SURROUND C

WINDOW SILL

Fig 96 PATTERN AND ASSEMBLY FOR BEDROOM WINDOW AND
WINDOW-SILL

With the door fitted in position, cut and fix the inner door-frame into the door opening so that when the door is butted against this frame, it is flush with the front edge of the outer door-frame. The door should be painted before it is fixed in place – we used Humbrol enamel paint and applied two coats of ivory gloss over one coat of matt – sanded between coats. Paint the door-frame and allow both door and frame to dry. Glue the hinges to the door with Superglue, then glue the completed door into the door frame, against the inner frame. The brass door-handle is from Jennifer's of Walsall (see stockists, p176).

WINDOW · To build up sufficient depth to make a window-sill, the window opening is faced with a frame of ³/₃₂ x ½in wood. The extra width protrudes on the outside of the room box. Cut the windowsill (the bottom of the frame) from the pattern (Fig 96) and glue in place. Cut the sides and top of the frame in ³/₃₂ x ½in wood and glue in place so that the front edges fit flush with the front edges of the window opening. This is frame A of Fig 96. An inner frame (Bi) is cut from ⅛in square wood and glued in place so that the back edges fit flush with frame A.

The window is glazed with thin perspex – we used 1mm Lexan sheet which is available from model shops. Cut the perspex to fit into the window opening against frame Bi and glue in place with a little UHU or similar glue. A second frame of ⅛ x ³/₁₆in wood (Bii) is cut and glued in place to butt against the perspex.

The mullions (D) are cut from ⅛ x ³/₁₆in wood and glued in place to the perspex and frame Bii to divide the window equally into three casements. Each casement is framed with ¹/₁₆in wood, glued to the perspex – frame C as shown on the pattern.

The window frame should be painted at this stage – before the glazing bars are fitted – and also paint a length of ¹/₁₆in square strip to make the glazing bars. When the paint is dry, cut the glazing bars and fix in place with glue or double-sided Sellotape (see Chapter 9 – instructions for the Attic window.)

The door and window are both framed with commercial architrave mouldings from Hobbys, (see magazines, p175), cut to fit with mitred corners, painted and glued in place, around the door and window. Note that the architrave around the door is cut to fit level with the bottom of the door-frame, leaving sufficient clearance for the step.

CHIMNEY-BREAST · The chimney-breast is made from ⅛in plywood (see Fig 97). Cut a triangular support from ³/₈in plywood and glue to the floor in the back right-hand corner of the room. Cut the chimney-breast, chamfer both side edges to 45° and glue in place to the support and walls.

FLOOR · The floor is planked with pre-glued iron-on veneer which is available from DIY shops. Cut ½in strips of veneer and iron onto the floor as described in Chapter 9. We used oak veneer, stained after fixing, with walnut wood-stain.

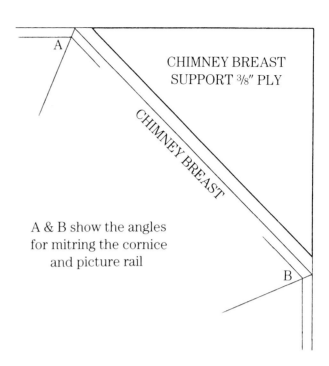

Fig 97 PATTERN FOR CHIMNEY-BREAST

CHIMNEY BREAST SUPPORT ³/₈" PLY

A & B show the angles for mitring the cornice and picture rail

STEP · The step is a block of balsa wood, faced with ⅛in thick oak, stained to match the floor. Cut a ½in thick balsa block 3½ x 1³/₈in. Face one long and one short side of the block with oak, mitring the corner to fit. The top over-hangs the block on the faced sides by ⅛in. Cut pieces as shown in Fig 98 and glue in place. Glue the sides and un-derside of the step and fit in place in the left-hand back corner of the room.

Polish the floor and step at this stage – we used two coats of beeswax polish, well buffed.

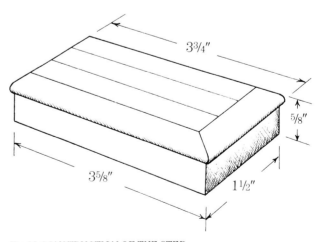

Fig 98 CONSTRUCTION OF THE STEP

Plate 25 THE BEDROOM – UNFURNISHED

CEILING · Cut the top to fit perfectly by turning the room upside-down and tracing around it onto ³⁄₈in plywood. Cut and sand, glue and pin, the top to the top of the walls.

SKIRTING, CORNICE AND PICTURE-RAIL · We used commercial mouldings from Hobby's. Cut the skirting, paint and glue it in place, trimming as necessary to fit against the step. Mark the line of the picture-rail on the walls in pencil and glue the pre-painted picture-rail in place. Cut and glue the cornice to the top of the walls and the ceiling. See Chapter 5 for full instructions. Fig 97 shows the angle of the mitres to be cut to fit skirting, picture-rail and cornice across the chimney-breast. Note that the skirting butts against each side of the fireplace, so the fireplace should be fitted, but not fixed, before the skirting is glued in place.

DECORATING · The ceiling and the top of the wall (between the picture-rail and cornice) were papered with lining paper, and the ceiling, cornice and top of the walls were painted with two coats of magnolia emulsion paint with a matt finish. (It is easier to do if you turn the room upside-down.) The walls are sized, then papered with a commercial dolls' house wallpaper, applied with wallpaper paste. The fireplace surround was painted with Humbrol enamel paint, and the fireplace was glued to the chimney-breast. The outside of the room box was painted with three coats of silk finish emulsion paint in smokey-blue, sanded thoroughly between coats.

The front edges were faced with ³⁄₈ x ¹⁄₈in wood-strip, stained with walnut wood-stain and with mitred corners and glued in place with impact adhesive. Finish the frame by sanding thoroughly, then French polish and beeswax.

CURTAINS · The curtains are made from printed cotton and hung from a pole made from a thin hollow brass rod (from model shops) with a brass door handle glued into each end. The rod is suspended from small brass eyes, screwed into the wall.

To make the curtains, choose suitably lightweight pure cotton fabric – man-made fibres will not crease or hang well. Cut the curtains a little wider than the window and seal all edges with Fraycheck. Fold, glue and press narrow hems down both sides and a slightly wider hem at the bottom. Turn and press a ¹⁄₂in hem at the top. Run two rows of small gathering stitches through the top hem and pull up the gathers to draw the curtains to the finished width required; fasten off the gathering threads. With strong thread, oversew the pole to the back of the curtains at the gathers. Working on the ironing-board, damp the curtains and pin them into folds. Hold a steam iron just above, but not touching the curtains, then leave them pinned on the ironing-board until they are thoroughly dry. Push the ends of the brass rod through the eye hooks and glue the door handles into the ends of the rod. Adjust

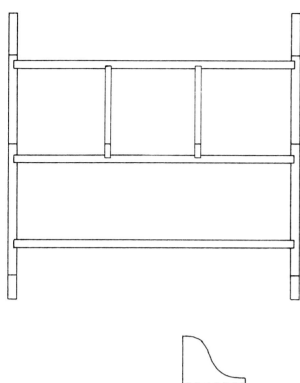

the curtains so that they hang to each side of the window and the small frill at the top stands upright.

LIGHTS · The room is lit with two brass and glass wall-lights and a copper tape system from Wood 'n Wool Miniatures. We drilled holes through the walls and ran the copper tape on the outside of the room box.

FURNITURE · All the furniture described here is made in 'real' wood – the patterns are not suitable for obeche. Choose your wood carefully, paying special attention to the size and pattern of the grain. In this scale, only fine-grained timber will produce the best results. We have noted the wood we have used for each piece, but other woods may be used as you prefer, particularly in the case of the pine pieces where it might be difficult to obtain wood with a suitably fine grain – cherry or spruce might be a better alternative.

Full instructions follow for making each piece of furniture. You may also find it helpful to consult Chapter 1. All pieces have been finished with three coats of dilute French polish, lightly sanded between coats, and two coats of pure beeswax polish, well buffed (see also pp25–6). If you prefer an 'old pine' finish, the piece should be stained with a light coat of thinned light oak stain before polishing.

WALL-SHELVES · The wall-shelves (Fig 99) are made of pine. Cut two oblong pieces for the sides and make the grooves to receive the shelves on the shaper table before you cut the shaped sides. Cut three shelves and two shelf dividers. Cut grooves in the top and middle shelves to receive the shelf dividers. Stain if required and French polish the pieces before assembly. All pieces are assembled together: glue the dividers into the shelves and the shelves into the sides, ensuring that the assembly is square and lies flat on the work surface. Apply wax polish after assembly.

TOWEL RAIL · The towel rail (Fig 100) is made of satin walnut. Cut four 4in square blanks for the uprights. Because of the small size of these pieces, it is not practicable to use the four-prong drive centre on the lathe. Therefore, roughly round off ³⁄₈in from one end of each piece and chuck this into a Jacob's chuck, then turn ³⁄₈in on the tail stock end of the piece. Remove the piece from the lathe and reverse it so that the turned end is held in the Jacob's chuck. Proceed with the turning as shown on the diagram. Note that pegs are turned at each end for fixing into the feet and arched tops. Drill ¹⁄₁₆in diameter holes in the square sections of the uprights to receive the rails.

Cut two feet and two arched tops as shown. We suggest that the arched top is turned on the lathe and cut in half to make these pieces. Drill holes in the feet and arched tops to receive the uprights and top rail. Glue and assemble the uprights into the feet and arched tops.

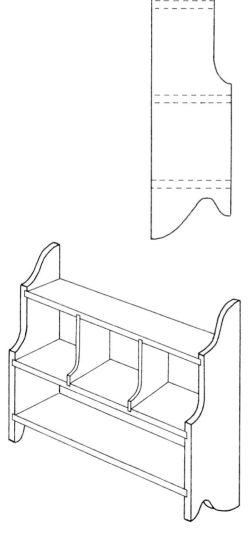

Fig 99 PATTERN AND ASSEMBLY FOR WALL-SHELVES

Fig 100 PATTERN FOR TOWEL RAIL

ROUND SECTION

SQUARE SECTION

BACK FRIEZE

(a)

(b)

SHAPING THE TOP WITH THE SHAPER
TABLE AND RIFFLER FILE

Fig 101 PATTERN AND CONSTRUCTION DETAILS FOR SMALL
TABLE

Prepare five ¹⁄₁₆in diameter rails. This is done most easily by whittling the rails from ¹⁄₁₆in square wood, sanding to a fine finish. Glue the rails into the ends, ensuring that the towel rail stands square and upright on the work surface. Stain and polish as required. Lengths of crêpe bandage and cotton tape have been used here for towels.

SMALL TABLE · The table (Fig 101) is made of mahogany.

Cut four 3½in blanks for the legs and turn these as shown on the diagram. Using the shaper table, cut mortises in the top of the legs to receive the frieze pieces, and use a ¹⁄₁₆in drill to make holes in the bottom of the legs to receive the stretchers.

Cut four frieze pieces, using a fret-saw for the curved edges on the front and side friezes; the back frieze is cut plain as shown on the diagram. Use the shaper table to cut a ¹⁄₃₂in deep decorative groove on the front and side friezes.

Cut four stretchers, ensuring that these are exactly the same length as the corresponding frieze pieces (ignore the tenons). Drill ¹⁄₁₆in diameter holes to a depth of ⅛in

centrally in each end of each stretcher. Prepare pegs to fit into these holes so that they protrude by ³⁄₃₂in and glue them in place (see Fig 101a). Round off the top edge of each stretcher.

Assemble the two table ends by gluing the frieze and the stretcher into the legs, ensuring that the assembly is square. When dry, glue the longer stretchers and friezes in place.

Cut the rectangular table-top and use the shaper table and flat riffler file to cut the moulded edge (see Fig 101b). Glue the table-top onto the leg assembly. Stain and polish as required.

CHEST-OF-DRAWERS · The chest-of-drawers (Fig 102) is made of pine. To make the carcase, first cut two side pieces and mark the positions of the dividers and the back as shown on the pattern. Cut grooves on these marks using the shaper table.

Fig 102 PATTERN FOR CHEST-OF-DRAWERS

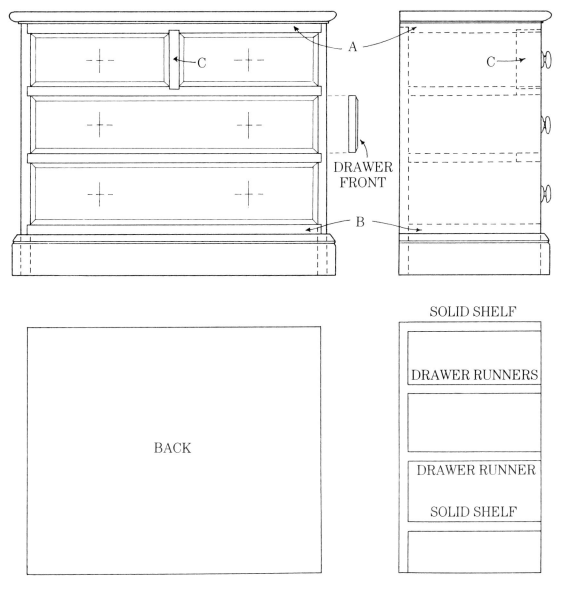

DRAWER FRONT

BACK

SOLID SHELF

DRAWER RUNNERS

DRAWER RUNNER

SOLID SHELF

Cut the under-top (A) and the bottom divider (B). Note that the under-top extends the full width of the side and that the back edge is grooved to receive the back. The bottom divider is cut to butt against the back. Cut a ¼in long groove, centrally on the underside of the under-top to receive the upright drawer divider (C). Cut the back as shown on the pattern.

Assemble the carcase by gluing the under-top (A) and the bottom divider (B) into the sides, and gluing the back into the recess formed by the sides and top (see Fig 103a).

Cut a strip of wood (A) ⅛ x ¼in and glue this beneath the bottom divider so that the front edges are flush (see Fig 103b). This forms a support for the plinth front.

Cut lengths of ¼in wide wood to make the drawer runners. Cut three pieces for each drawer runner and glue in place into the grooves in the sides of the carcase as shown in Fig 103b. Note that the top-drawer runner has a central groove to correspond with the under-top.

Cut the upright drawer divider (see Fig 102 (C)) and glue into place, checking that it fits easily without distorting the drawer runner.

Cut the top as shown on the pattern and use the shaper table and riffler file to shape the moulded edge on the sides and front. Glue the top onto the carcase, lining up the back edges and clamp in place until dry.

To make the plinth, prepare an 8in length of wood and use the shaper table and riffler file to shape the top edge. Cut the lengths and glue the plinth to the sides and front of the carcase with mitred corners as shown in Fig 103b.

Cut four drawer fronts to fit the drawer spaces. Chamfer the four edges of each drawer front and assemble the drawers as described on pp23–4).

Stain and polish the carcase and the drawer fronts as required.

We have used small drawer knobs with pegs turned from yew which are glued into holes drilled into the drawer fronts.

WASHSTAND · The turned parts of the washstand (Fig 104) are made of spruce, the rest of pine. Cut four 3½in blanks for the legs, chuck these onto the four-pronged drive centre and turn as shown on the pattern. Use the shaper table to cut mortises in the back legs to receive the back and side frieze pieces and in the front legs to receive the side friezes only. Using a ¹⁄₁₆in bit, drill holes in each leg to receive the stretchers.

Cut two 2½in blanks for the stretchers. Because of the small size of these pieces, it is not practicable to use the four-prong drive centre on the lathe. Therefore, roughly round off ³⁄₈in from one end of each piece and chuck this into a Jacob's chuck, then turn ³⁄₈in on the tail stock end of each piece. Remove the piece from the lathe and reverse it so that the turned end is held in the Jacob's chuck. Proceed with the turning as shown on the pattern. Cut two side and one back frieze pieces from the pattern. Assemble the two washstand ends by gluing the side

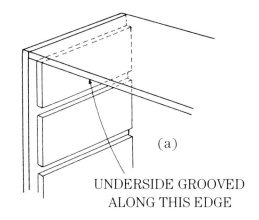

(a)

UNDERSIDE GROOVED
ALONG THIS EDGE

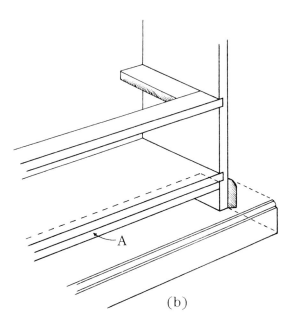

(b)

Fig 103 CONSTRUCTION DETAILS FOR CHEST-OF-DRAWERS

friezes and stretchers into the legs. Check that each assembly is square and allow to dry thoroughly.

Cut two ⁵⁄₁₆in wide drawer-runner supports (Fig 105a – A) to fit below the side friezes. Round off one long edge on each piece and glue below the side friezes so that the rounded edge projects slightly to form the decorative beading.

Cut two drawer-runners (B), ⁵⁄₁₆ x ¹⁄₁₆in, the same length as the drawer-runner supports. Glue in place to the drawer-runner supports and side friezes (see Fig 105b).

Glue the back frieze into the end leg assemblies, ensuring that the construction is square and rests flat on the work surface.

Cut the rectangular top from the pattern and glue onto the leg assembly. Note that the top overhangs a little at the back edge.

Cut four pieces for the drawer frame (see Fig 104 (C)), glue the top piece between the legs and to the underside of the top. Glue the side pieces to butt beneath the top

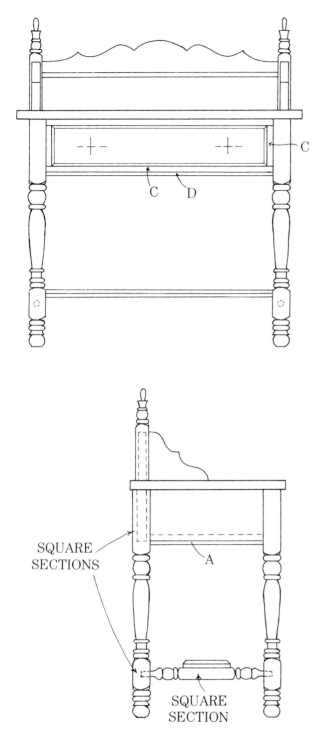

this beading is in place, the bottom of the drawer opening and the drawer-runners should be at the same level.

Cut the drawer front to fit the drawer space and assemble the drawer as described on pp23–4.

Cut a shelf to extend to the outer edges of the side stretchers. Chamfer the top edges and glue in place across the stretchers.

To make the splash-back, cut two sides and a back from the pattern with a fret-saw (see Fig 104). Mortise and tenon joints have been used to assemble the splash-back. These joints need to be very small and you may prefer to butt joint these pieces as this will provide adequate strength once the splash-back is glued to the top of the washstand.

Cut two 2in blanks for the posts and chuck these onto the lathe, using the same method as described above for the side stretchers.

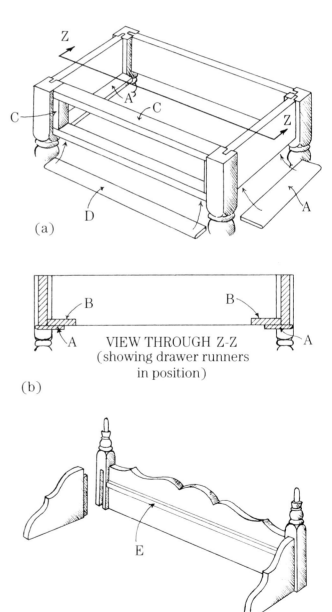

SQUARE SECTIONS

SQUARE SECTION

Fig 104 PATTERN FOR WASHSTAND

(a)

VIEW THROUGH Z-Z
(showing drawer runners
in position)

(b)

piece and the bottom piece to butt beneath the side pieces.

Cut a beading piece (Fig 104 (D)), ³/₁₆in wide. Round off the front edge and glue beneath the bottom-drawer frame piece so that the rounded edge projects slightly to match the side pieces.

The drawer opening is faced with very fine wood-strip, with the front edges rounded off and glued in place with these rounded front edges projecting slightly to form a decorative beading around the drawer opening. When

Fig 105 CONSTRUCTION DETAILS FOR WASHSTAND

Assemble the splash-back by gluing the back between the posts and the sides to the posts, checking that the assembly is square and stands straight on the work surface. Glue the splash-back to the top of the washstand. A very fine strip of wood is glued to the back of the splash-back (Fig 105 (E)) as a decorative trim.

Stain and polish the washstand as required. We have used small drawer handles with pegs, turned from yew, which are glued into holes drilled in the drawer fronts.

DRESSING-TABLE · The turned parts of the dressing-table (Fig 106) are made of spruce, the rest of pine.

Cut four $3\frac{1}{2}$in blanks for the legs. Chuck these onto the four-prong drive centre and turn as shown on the pattern. Use the shaper table to cut mortises in the back legs to receive the back and side frieze pieces and in the front legs to receive the side friezes only. Using a $\frac{1}{16}$in bit, drill holes in each leg to receive the stretchers.

Cut two $2\frac{1}{2}$in blanks for the stretchers. Because of the small size of these pieces, it is not practicable to use the four-prong drive centre on the lathe. Therefore, roughly round off $\frac{3}{8}$in from one end of each piece and chuck this

into a Jacob's chuck. Then turn $\frac{3}{8}$in on the tail stock end of each piece. Remove the piece from the lathe and reverse it so that the turned end is held in the Jacob's chuck. Proceed with the turning as shown on the pattern. Cut two side and one back frieze pieces from the pattern. Assemble the two dressing-table ends by gluing the side friezes and stretchers into the legs. Check that each assembly is square and allow them to dry thoroughly.

Cut three $\frac{5}{16}$in wide drawer-runner supports (Fig 107b – A; see also Fig 105a) to fit below the side and back friezes. Round off one long edge on each piece and glue the side pieces below the side friezes so that the rounded edge projects slightly to form the decorative beading. Glue the back frieze into the leg assemblies, ensuring that the construction is square and rests flat on the work surface.

Glue the back drawer runner support (Ai) to the underside of the back frieze. If necessary, trim the corners of this piece to fit well.

The drawer-runner (B) is cut as one solid piece from the pattern (Fig 107c). Glue the drawer runner to rest on the back and side drawer-runner supports.

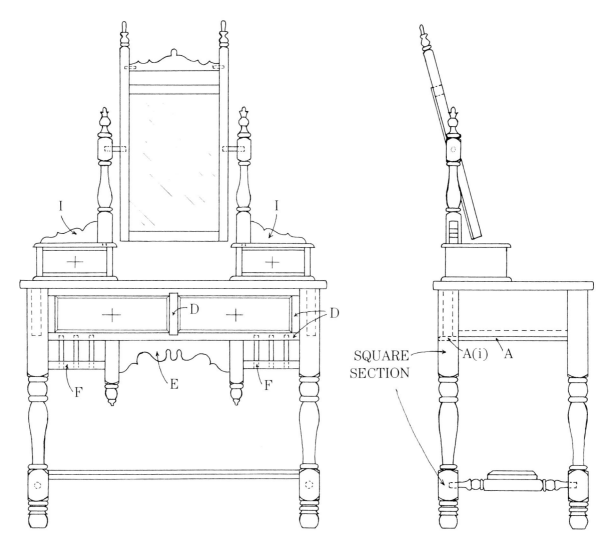

Fig 106 PATTERN FOR DRESSING-TABLE

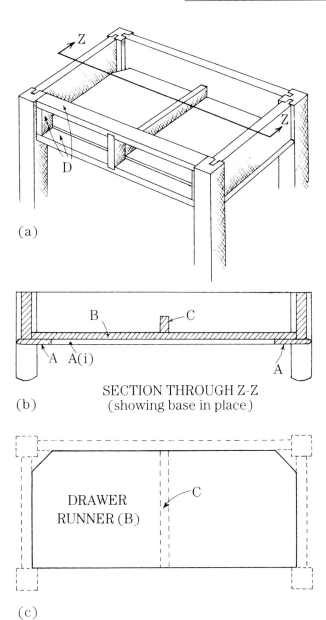

(a)

(b)

SECTION THROUGH Z-Z
(showing base in place)

(c)

Fig 107 ASSEMBLY FOR DRESSING-TABLE

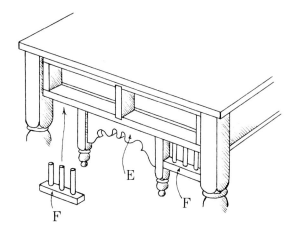

Fig 108 DECORATIVE TRIM FOR DRESSING-TABLE

ings should be at the same level as the drawer runner.

Cut the drawer fronts to fit the drawer spaces and assemble the drawers as described on pp23–4.

To make the decorative trim under the drawers as shown in Fig 108, cut two 2in long blanks for the posts. Chuck these onto the lathe using the same method as described above for the stretchers and turn as shown on the pattern. Note that the posts have ^{1}/16in pegs turned to fit into the underside of the drawer frame. Cut mortises on the posts to receive the central rail (E).

Using a fret-saw, cut a rectangular piece for the central rail and cut the tenons before the curved lower edge is shaped. Glue the central rail into the posts.

Drill holes in the underside of the drawer frame to receive the pegs of the posts and glue the central rail and posts in place.

Cut two rails (F) to fit snugly between the posts and the legs. Mark and drill three holes through both pieces to receive the spindles. Use the rails, pushed into place under the drawer frame, as a guide to drill through the holes in the rails into the underside of the drawer frame to receive the spindles. Cut or turn six spindles and glue these into the rails. Glue the top of the spindles into the holes in the drawer frame (Fig 108).

Cut a shelf to extend to the outer edges of the side stretchers. Chamfer the top edges and glue in place across the stretchers.

To make the mirror and drawer unit (Fig 109) assemble the drawer boxes first. For each box, cut a base from the pattern and round off the four top edges. Cut an inner base (G) and glue onto the base as shown in Fig 109b. Cut two sides and a back and glue these around the inner base. Cut the top, round off the top edges as for the base and glue onto the sides and back.

Cut a small top-edge piece (H) and glue to the underside of the top so that it is flush with the sides and completes a frame for the drawer.

Cut the drawer fronts to fit the drawer spaces and assemble the drawers, using the simple method described on pp23–4. Do not glue the boxes to the dressing-table at this stage.

Cut the drawer divider (C) the same depth as the drawer-runner and glue in place as shown on the pattern.

Cut the rectangular top from the pattern and glue onto the leg assembly. Note that the top overhangs a little at the back edge.

Cut five pieces for the drawer frame (see Fig 106 (D)). Cut grooves in the longer pieces to receive the central drawer divider. Glue the top piece between the legs and to the underside of the top. Glue the side pieces to butt beneath the top piece. Glue the central divider in place and at the same time glue the bottom piece to butt beneath the side pieces.

The drawer openings are faced with very fine wood-strip with the front edges rounded off and glued in place with these rounded front edges projecting slightly to form a decorative beading around the drawer openings. With this beading in place the bottom of the drawer open-

Plate 26 BEDROOM FURNITURE

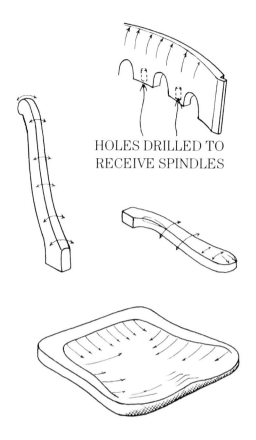

HOLES DRILLED TO
RECEIVE SPINDLES

Fig 112 DETAILS OF SHAPING FOR CHAIR PARTS

Cut two back stands from the pattern, rounding the front edges as shown in Fig 112. Drill holes with a 1/16in bit into the lower ends of the stands to a depth of 1/8in to receive pegs which will fit the stands into the seat. Before fitting the pegs, make careful references to Fig 111 to determine the correct angle at which the stands fit onto the seat. Trim the bottom of the stands to this angle, then cut and glue the pegs in place, leaving 3/32in protruding. Drill 1/16in diameter holes into the seat to receive the back stand pegs. Note that these holes are drilled to correspond with the angle of the stands. Do not glue the stand pegs into the seat at this stage.

Cut the upper and lower rails from the pattern. Note that both pieces have tenons at both ends which do not follow the curved profile of the rails. Cut the arches with a fret-saw and clean up with a round needle file. Drill fine holes between the arches in the top rail to receive the back spindles. Refer to the pattern to determine the angle at which these holes are drilled. (Do not drill corresponding holes in the bottom rail.)

Cut mortises in the stands with a craft knife, metal rule and watchmaker's 'chisel' to receive the tenons in the rails. (Check that the mortises are cut on the inner sides of both the left- and right-hand stands.)

Dry-fit the rails between the stands and the stands into the seat to ensure that each piece fits squarely and that the stands are symmetrical and adjust if necessary. Glue

the rails into the stands and the stands into the seat and allow to dry thoroughly.

Cut four 1½in round blanks for the back spindles and turn as shown on the pattern. Note that the top of each spindle is turned to a length and diameter to fit into the holes in the underside of the top rail. Glue the spindles into the top rail and ease them into position to rest on the bottom rail.

Cut a pair of arms from the pattern and shape the top edges as shown in Fig 112.

Cut grooves in the stands to receive the arms, using a craft knife.

Cut four 2in round blanks for the arm spindles and turn two pairs as shown on the pattern, ensuring that sufficient length is left at each end to peg the spindles into the seat and the arms. Drill holes into the seat at the places marked and into the underside of the arms to receive the spindles as shown on the pattern. Note that the spindles project both forward and outward from the seat and the receiving holes should be drilled accordingly. Glue the spindles into the seat and glue the arms onto the spindles and into the stands.

Prepare four 2½in round blanks for the legs and three 2½in blanks for the stretchers. Turn the legs and stretchers as shown on the pattern, ensuring that the top of the legs and both ends of the stretchers are extended sufficiently to peg into place. Using the guideline on the underside of the seat, mark the position of the legs. Refer to the pattern to determine the angles and drill holes to receive the legs. Glue the front legs into the seat and allow to dry thoroughly. Mark and drill holes for the side stretchers in the front and back legs and holes in the side stretchers for the centre stretcher. Glue the side stretchers into the front and back legs and the back legs into the seat as one operation. Apply a little glue to the holes in the side stretchers and ease the centre stretcher into place. Trim the bottom of each leg with a craft knife so that the legs rest flat on the work surface. Stain and polish the chair as required.

ACCESSORIES · The Pre-Raphaelite pictures on the walls were cut from a Tate Gallery catalogue and framed with mouldings from Hobby's. Patterns and instructions for the dressing-gown, hat, gloves and handbag can be found in Chapter 7.

The bed has a pair of cotton sheets, two pillows and a fine wool blanket. The frilled bedspread is made of silk and the lace spread from strips of old lace which are whipped together. The very fine blue and white porcelain vase and plate were made by Carol Lodder. The 'Coalport' castle on the mantel is from The Mulberry Bush, the baskets from C & D Crafts, and the tiny ornaments and the slippers from Dorking Dolls' House Gallery. The artist's palette and paints are from Mini Mansions and the pencil box, drawing-book and the jug and basin are from The Singing Tree. The beautiful 'Aubusson' carpet is from Polly Flinders (see Stockists).

11 THE FARMHOUSE KITCHEN

This project is designed for the more experienced furniture-maker, although the room set with its small extension for the stairs is fairly simple to build. The stairs will require careful measuring and cutting; if you prefer, the room may be made without the stairs extension by cutting the base and top straight across the back edge. The stairs door could be replaced with a false door as in the 'Edwardian Bedroom' (see p133) or it could be omitted. The room has a large chimney-breast which has been built to accommodate a commercial kitchen range (from The Singing Tree – see list of stockists, p176), a non-opening window and two opening doors. We have used flagstone flooring made by Sussex Crafts (also available from The Singing Tree) but if you prefer to make your own flagstones in Das or similar clay, see the instructions on p127 for bricks and stones. The room box is built of 3/8in plywood.

The furniture is made in pine, yew and cherry, using authentic furniture-making methods and the full range of tools discussed in Chapter 1. Joints may be cut by hand if you do not have a shaper table, or omitted in favour of butt joints.

ROOM SET

Referring to Fig 113, cut a base (B), a back (D) and two sides (A and C) from 3/8in plywood. Mark the position of the window and door openings on the back and the door opening on the side (A) and cut out with a fret-saw. Sand the edges of the cut-outs to a smooth finish.

Glue and pin the left-hand side (with door opening) to the outside of the base. Glue and pin the back onto the base and to the side. Glue and pin the other side to the outside of the base and to the back wall above the door opening.

Cut the stairs extension back wall (F). Glue and pin outside the base and to the side wall.

Do not fix the top or stairs extension wall (E) at this stage.

STAIRS · Before the stairs are built, the stairs door opening should be framed (Fig 114). Face the left-hand side and top of the door opening with 1/8in wood-strip. Cut a length of wood 3/8 x 1/4in to form the right-hand door post to complete the door-frame. The door will be hinged to this post, so simply dry-fit it in place at this stage. Cut and fit a 1/8in square inner frame to the top and left side of the door opening and to the separate right-hand door post. This frame should be fitted fractionally more than 1/8in back from the front edge of the door opening.

To make the stairs (Fig 115), each step is cut separately, either in 5/8in thick balsa wood or in 1/2in thick balsa wood faced with 1/8in obeche wood to build up a thickness of 5/8in. The steps are cut to cover the area of the stairwell, so that, assembled, they form a solid block. Points A and B on the pattern apply to every tread and points C-M apply to the individual treads – ie, for the bottom step, cut the pattern A-B-C-D and for the second step cut the pattern A-B-C-F-D. Points A-D and D-C allow for the fitting of a skirting-board on the side and back walls of the stairwell. Cut pieces of 3/32in thick wood, 3in high, to fit against the side and back walls to use as spacers while the stairs are cut and fitted. Working from the bottom step upwards, cut each step and face the front edge with a riser of 3/32in wood (we have used pine). The outside edges of each riser should be angled to follow the line of the steps as shown on the pattern. Assemble and glue the steps so that they fit snugly into the stairwell, against the spacers and wall D. Remove the stairs to fit the treads. Cut treads to fit each step in 1/8in thick wood so that the front edge overhangs the riser by 3/32in, and round off the front edges before you glue the treads in place. Note that the nose on the first step must be trimmed to fit around the door frame and that the corner D on the third step must be trimmed to fit into the corner of the stairwell. Sand the stairs thoroughly, hollowing the centre of the treads if required to simulate wear, and stain and polish before the stairs are glued in place. (If you intend to paint the stairwell walls, do so before the skirting-boards and stairs are fixed in place. Wallpaper may be applied after the skirting-boards are fixed.)

THE FARMHOUSE KITCHEN

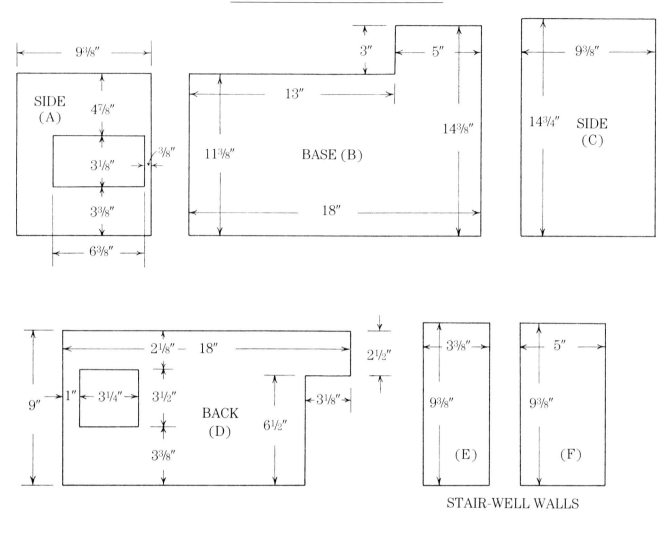

SIDE (A)

9³⁄₈″

4⁷⁄₈″

3¹⁄₈″

³⁄₈″

3³⁄₈″

6³⁄₈″

BASE (B)

3″   5″

13″

11³⁄₈″

14³⁄₈″

18″

SIDE (C)

9³⁄₈″

14³⁄₄″

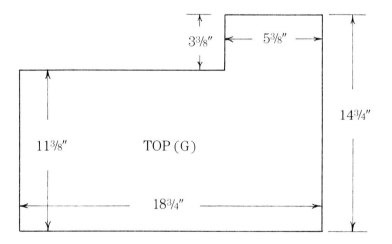

BACK (D)

2¹⁄₈″ – 18″

2¹⁄₂″

9″

1″   3¹⁄₄″

3¹⁄₂″

3³⁄₈″

6¹⁄₂″

3¹⁄₈″

STAIR-WELL WALLS

3³⁄₈″

9³⁄₈″

(E)

5″

9³⁄₈″

(F)

3³⁄₈″   5³⁄₈″

11³⁄₈″   TOP (G)

14³⁄₄″

18³⁄₄″

Fig 113 PATTERN FOR THE KITCHEN ROOM-SET

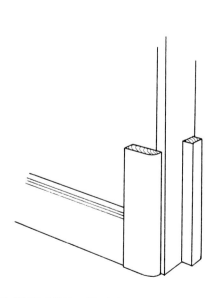

Fig 114 DETAIL OF FRAMING AND ARCHITRAVE FOR THE STAIRS DOOR

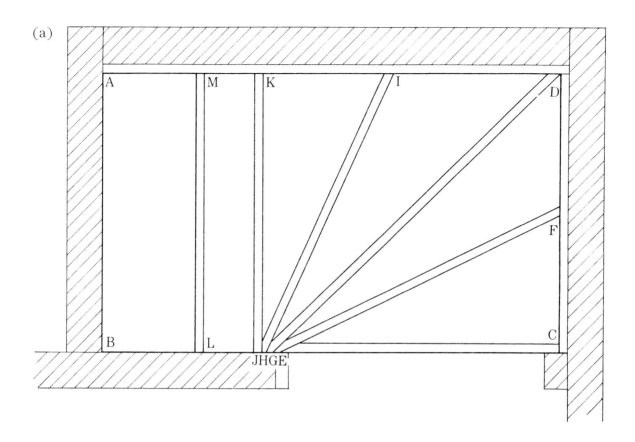

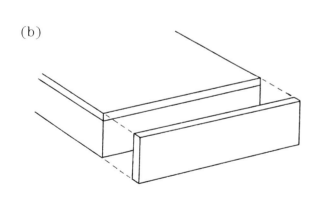

Fig 115 PATTERN AND ASSEMBLY FOR STAIRS: (A) LAYOUT OF
STAIRS AND SKIRTING-BOARD (NOSES OMITTED); (B)
BUILDING UP AND FACING THE STAIRS; (C) ASSEMBLING THE
STAIRS AND FIXING THE TREADS

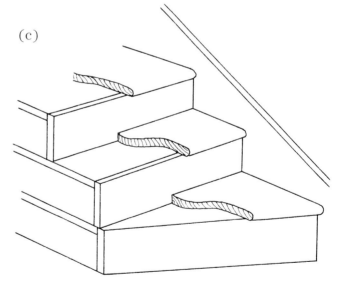

Overleaf:
Plate 27 THE FARMHOUSE KITCHEN

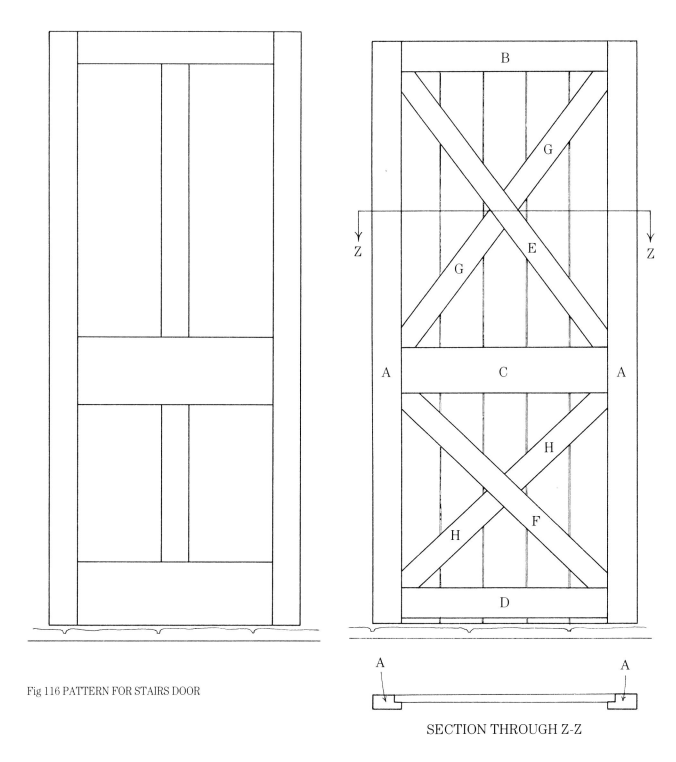

Fig 116 PATTERN FOR STAIRS DOOR

SECTION THROUGH Z-Z

Fig 117 PATTERN FOR BACK DOOR

To make the skirting-board for the right-hand side wall, cut a piece of pine $^3/_2$in thick, to fit the width of the side wall with the top edge angled to follow the line of the stairs – approximately $^1/_4$in above the nose of the treads (Fig 115c). Sand, stain and polish this piece and glue it to the side of the stairs. To make the skirting for the back wall, cut a strip of wood 1$^1/_2$in wide to fit behind the stairs. Mark the outline of the stairs onto the skirting piece. Draw the top line of the skirting to follow the angle of the stairs, approximately $^1/_4$in above the nose of each tread so that it lines up with the top of the skirting on the side walls. Cut along this marked line and sand, stain and polish the piece. Fit the skirting in place behind the stairs and mark the top edge onto the wall. Remove the stairs and glue the skirting to the wall, then glue the bottom of the stairs and fit them in place. (Wallpaper the stairwell walls if required.)

Cut the stairwell wall (E) and glue and pin outside the base to the stairwell back wall (F) and back wall (D).

STAIRS DOOR · The door is made of $^1/_{16}$in thick wood (we have used spruce) panelled with $^1/_2$in spruce on both sides.

Note that the door must be cut to allow clearance for the flooring. Fig 116 allows $^1/_8$in clearance, sufficient for stone flags.

The door post (which completes the door frame) should be fitted in place and held temporarily with a little glue while the door is measured. Cut the door so that it fits the door opening with a fractional clearance all around and clearance for the floor at the bottom. Sand thoroughly and cut and fit panelling pieces to both sides as shown on the pattern. Cut recesses for the hinges and glue the hinges in place. Hold the door in place in the frame and mark the position of the hinges on the door post. Remove the door post and cut recesses for the hinges. Glue the hinges to the door post. (Paint the door and the door post before the door post is glued in place.)

The door is framed at the top and left-hand side with pine strip, $^5/_{16}$ x $^1/_{16}$in, with the inner edges rounded and a mitred corner (see Fig 114). Glue the door post (with the hinged door) in place. Use wedges butted against the left-hand side of the door frame to apply pressure to the post as the glue dries.

BACK DOOR · The door is made of pine (Fig 117). Frame the door opening with $^1/_8$ x $^3/_8$in wood-strip. Make a second frame of $^1/_8$in square wood-strip, $^1/_{16}$in from the inner edge. Cut a cardboard template to fit the door opening with fractional clearance all around and clearance for the floor at the bottom. Use the template to check measurements as you build the door.

To make the frame, cut two pieces (A) for the uprights from the pattern (see section through Z-Z.) Using the shaper table, cut a groove along the full length of each piece. Prepare the top of the frame (B) in the same way. From the top end of each upright, cut away the lip that is formed by the grooving to receive the top (see Fig 118a).

Dry-fit the top between the uprights and check the overall width of the door against the template; trim if necessary and glue the top between the uprights.

Cut planking from either a solid, scored piece or by butt jointing lengths together to fit into the frame so that the planking and the frame are flush. Glue the planking into the frame (Fig 118b).

Cut the cross braces C and D (Fig 117) and glue in place to the inside of the door so that they are flush with the frame.

Cut the diagonal braces E and F to fit across the door and the pieces G and H to fit on either side of E and F and glue in place.

Cut recesses for the hinges in the door and glue the hinges in place. Fit the door and mark the hinges on the door frame; cut recesses and glue the hinges in place. (It is easier to paint the door and door frame before the door is hinged in place.) The door is framed with architrave in the same way as the stairs door.

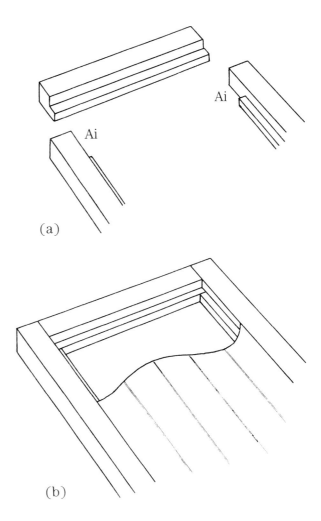

Fig 118 DETAILS OF CONSTRUCTION OF BACK DOOR

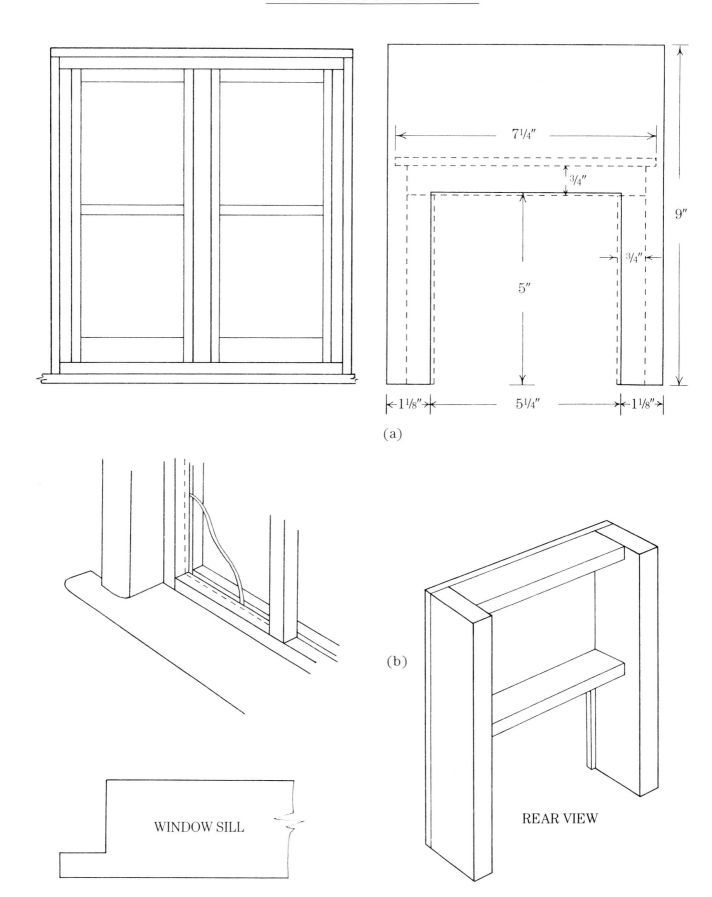

(a)

7¼"

¾"

9"

5"

¾"

1⅛"

5¼"

1⅛"

(b)

WINDOW SILL

REAR VIEW

Fig 119 PATTERN AND ASSEMBLY FOR WINDOW AND WINDOW SILL

Fig 120 PATTERN AND ASSEMBLY FOR CHIMNEY-BREAST

158

Fig 121 POSITION OF WALLS AND CHIMNEY-BREAST

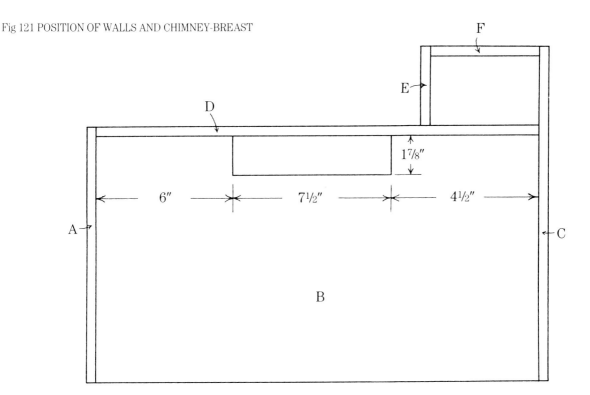

WINDOW · Although the dimensions are different, the window and windowsill are made in exactly the same way as the window in the Edwardian bedroom described on p137. The window is extended beyond the back wall to allow depth for the sill and framed with architrave to match the doors, although this frame is only ¼in wide (Fig 119).

CHIMNEY-BREAST · The chimney-breast is made from ⅛in plywood on a frame of 1¾ x 1in wood (Fig 120). Cut the chimney-breast front (Fig 120a) in plywood. Cut two frame uprights from 1¾in x 1in wood and glue and pin to the back of the plywood front. Cut two horizontal braces from scrap wood and glue between the uprights, to the front (Fig 120b).

Face the sides of the fireplace opening with ⅛in obeche wood so that the front edges are flush.

Glue the bottom and back edges of the chimney-breast and fit it in place on the back wall as shown in Fig 121.

CEILING · Cut the top to fit perfectly by turning the room upside down and tracing around it onto ⅜in plywood. Cut, sand and glue and pin the top to the top of the walls.

DECORATING · The stairwell is decorated with a commercial dolls' house wallpaper. The kitchen walls and ceiling are papered with lining paper and painted with two coats of matt-finish emulsion paint in cream for the walls and magnolia for the ceiling. The woodwork was painted with Humbrol matt-finish enamel paint – two shades mixed to make duck-egg green.

A decorative beam, cut from ¾ x ½in oak, cut roughly with a fret-saw and stained dark oak, was glued to the

ceiling on the window side of the chimney-breast. The hearth was tiled with tile-effect dolls' house paper, glued to a cardboard backing and the tiles scored with a blunt pointed tool. A hearthstone was cut from a roofing slate with a fret-saw and glued to the floor inside the hearth.

The fireplace surround (Fig 122) is cut from ⅛in thick pine, stained with medium-oak wood stain and glued in place so that the uprights overlap the tiled sides fractionally and the cross piece overhangs the opening. The

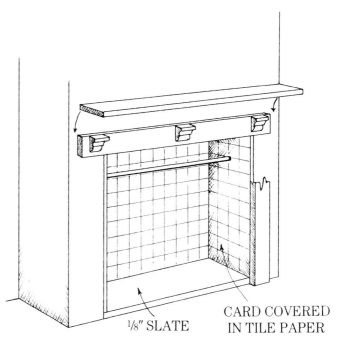

⅛" SLATE   CARD COVERED IN TILE PAPER

Fig 122 DETAIL OF FIREPLACE OPENING

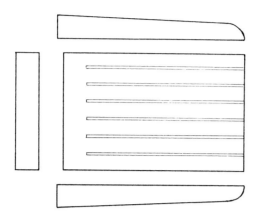

mantleshelf is ¾in deep and is supported on three ½in brackets cut from decorative wood moulding.

The flagstone flooring is glued to the floor with UHU. It is laid to fit up to the bottom stair in the stairs doorway and to the edge of the base in the back doorway, and fits to the walls all the way around the room.

The skirting-board (from Hobby's), which was sanded and painted before fitting, is glued to the wall, with mitred corners, to rest on top of the floor.

The outside of the room was painted with three coats of satin-finish emulsion paint in duck-egg green, sanded between coats. The front edges are framed with ⅜ x ⅛in wood-strip, stained with walnut wood stain and glued in place with mitred corners, with impact adhesive, French polished and waxed.

FITTINGS · The fire in the grate of the kitchen range is made in the same way as the one described on p61, and the range is glued to the wall and the hearthstone. The brass drying-rail is a length of ¹⁄₁₆in brass rod (from model shops), fitted and sprung into holes that have been drilled in both sides of the chimney-breast.

The glazed pottery sink from Sussex Crafts (see list of stockists, p177) is complete with waste-pipe and brass tap. The tap is glued into a hole drilled in the wall. The sink stands on brick piers made from ¼in balsa wood covered with Das bricks (see p127).

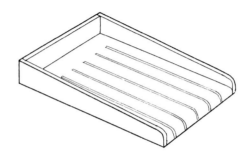

Fig 123 PATTERN FOR THE DRAINING-BOARD

DRAINING BOARD · To make the draining-board(s) (Fig 123), cut a base from ³⁄₂in obeche wood. Round off the front edge and score the grooves. Cut the sides and back from ¹⁄₁₆in obeche and glue around the base. Sand and stain with a light coat of light-oak wood stain. Glue small blocks of stained wood to the walls to support the draining-boards.

LIGHTING · We used a brass 'oil lamp' and the copper-tape wiring system from Wood 'n Wool Miniatures (see list of

Fig 124 PATTERN FOR THE TABLE

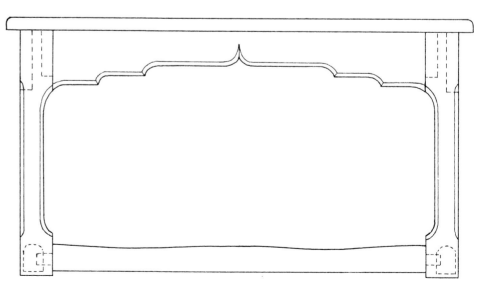

stockists, p177), who also produce an excellent booklet on the copper-tape method. The wires were fed through a hole drilled in the ceiling, and the copper tape was run on the outside of the room box. A slightly larger hole was drilled through the back wall above the stairs to feed a bulb through to light the stairwell.

FURNITURE · The furniture described in this chapter is made in pine, yew and cherry, although other woods may be used if you prefer. The woods we used for each piece are specified – all pieces were finished with French polish and beeswax. Choose woods carefully, paying particular attention to the size and pattern of the grain. It may be difficult to find pine with a suitably fine grain, but the dresser and table would be equally effective made in oak. Full instructions follow for each piece of furniture and you may also find it helpful to consult Chapter 1.

TABLE · The table (Fig 124) is made of pine. The friezes are tenoned into the legs so that the outer edges are flush. Careful measuring is therefore essential when cutting these joints (see Fig 125).

Cut four rectangles to make the friezes, but remember to cut them sufficiently long to form the tenons. Cut tenons at the end of each piece before you use the fret-saw to cut the shaped edges. Smooth the shaped edges with a needle file and abrasive paper, but do not chamfer at this stage.

Cut four legs from the pattern, but do not cut out the curved sections. Use the friezes to mark the positions of the mortises so that, when fitted, the front edges of legs and friezes will be flush. Cut the mortises using the shaper table. Dry-fit the longer friezes into the legs and mark the continuation of the curve onto each leg. Cut out the curved sections on the legs. Smooth the shaped edge with a needle file and abrasive paper, but do not chamfer at this stage.

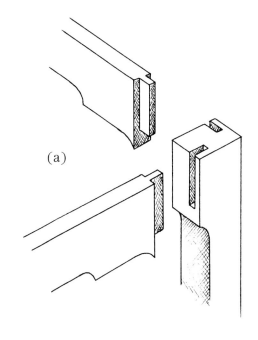

(a)

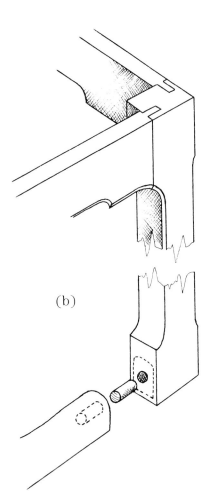

(b)

Fig 125 DETAILS OF CONSTRUCTION FOR THE TABLE

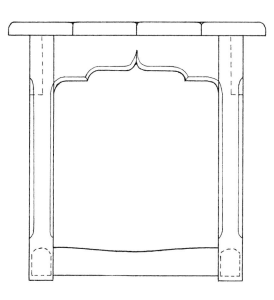

Plate 28 THE KITCHEN – UNFURNISHED

Cut two pairs of stretchers from the pattern, ensuring that they are exactly the same length as the friezes. Using a ⅛in drill bit, drill holes to a depth of ³⁄₁₆in in the ends of each stretcher to receive pegs. Drill corresponding holes into the table legs to a depth of ⅛in. Cut ⅛in diameter pegs and glue into the stretchers so that ⅛in protrudes. Round off the top edges of each stretcher and make a few hollow areas to simulate wear if required.

To assemble the table, glue the long stretchers and frieze pieces into the legs. Allow to dry thoroughly, then glue the short stretchers and friezes into the leg assemblies, checking that the assembly stands square on the work surface.

With a craft knife, needle file and abrasive paper, chamfer the outside edges of the legs and friezes as shown in Fig 124.

To make the top, cut four lengths of wood for planks, to overhang the leg assembly as shown on the pattern. Glue and butt the pieces together. When they are thoroughly dry, glue the top onto the leg assembly. Sand the edges slightly rounded, then thoroughly sand the top. Stain and polish as required.

DRESSER · The dresser is made of pine and the base and top are made separately (Figs 126-7).

To make the base, cut a top (A) and bottom (B) from the pattern. Use the shaper table to cut grooves to receive the sides and back (see Fig 126). Note that the grooves for the sides are ⅛in wide and the groove for the back is ³⁄₂in wide. Cut a groove ⅛in wide in the bottom to receive the upright divider (D), but do not cut a corresponding groove in the top.

Cut two sides from the pattern and use the shaper table to cut grooves ³⁄₂in wide to receive the back and the drawer support (C).

Cut the drawer support (C). Note that this is not the full depth of the side but is cut to butt against the back. Use the shaper table to cut a groove ⅛in wide across the underside of the drawer support to receive the upright divider (D) and a notch ⅛in wide and ¼in long in the upper side to receive the drawer divider (E) (see Fig 128).

Cut the upright divider (D) the same depth as the drawer support so that this also butts against the back.

Assemble the carcase by gluing the drawer support (C) into the sides so that the front edges are flush. Glue the sides into the bottom and at the same time, glue the upright divider (D) into the bottom and drawer support and glue the sides into the top (Fig 128). Check that the assembly is square and that all the front edges are flush, and allow to dry thoroughly.

Cut the back to fit into the recess made by the top, bottom and sides. This may be made in one piece with planking scored, or more realistically by butting ½in wide planks together. Glue the back in place.

Cut a piece of ³⁄₂in x ¼in wood to fit across the top of the drawer space (F). Cut a groove in the underside to correspond with the notch in the top of the drawer support and glue the piece in place, under the top, so that the edges are flush.

Cut the drawer divider (E) from ⅛ x ¼in wood and glue in place by easing it into the grooves.

Cut two frieze pieces (G) from the pattern in ³⁄₂in thick wood and glue in place under the drawer support. Note that these pieces are recessed slightly and not fitted flush to the front edges (Fig 129).

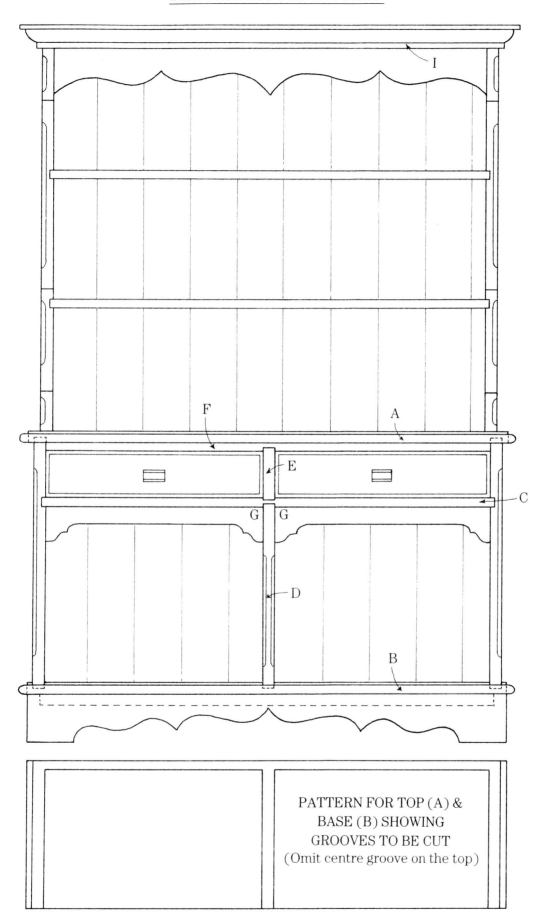

PATTERN FOR TOP (A) &
BASE (B) SHOWING
GROOVES TO BE CUT
(Omit centre groove on the top)

Fig 126 PATTERN FOR THE DRESSER (FRONT VIEW)

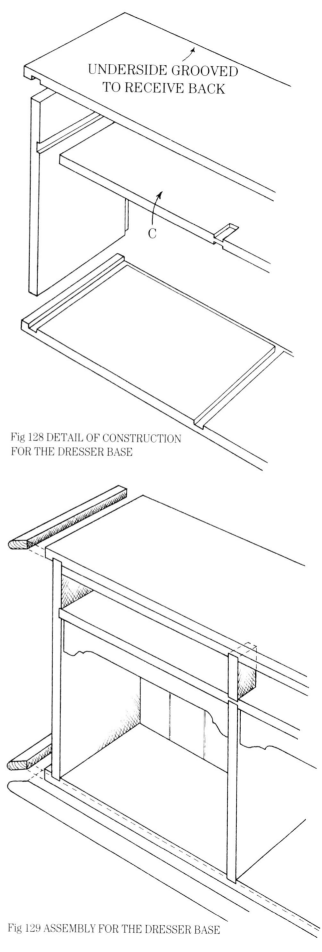

UNDERSIDE GROOVED
TO RECEIVE BACK

C

Fig 128 DETAIL OF CONSTRUCTION
FOR THE DRESSER BASE

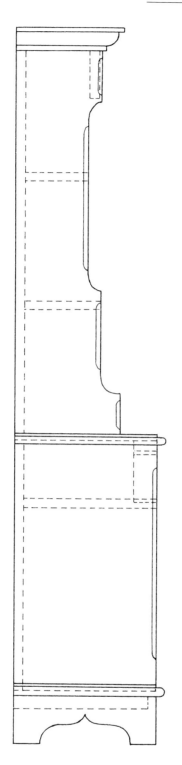

Fig 127 PATTERN FOR THE DRESSER (SIDE VIEW)

Fig 129 ASSEMBLY FOR THE DRESSER BASE

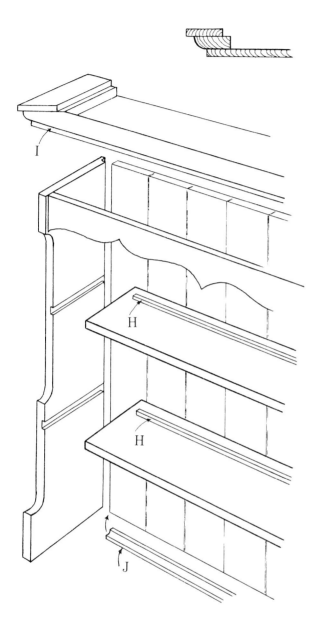

Fig 130 ASSEMBLY FOR THE DRESSER TOP

The front and side edges of the top and bottom are faced with a beading cut from ³/₃₂in wood. To make the beading, cut strips of wood ³/₃₂ x ⅛in wide and round off one edge. Glue these, making mitred corners, to the front and side edges of the top and bottom (Fig 129). Note that when the beading is glued in place, a lip is formed against the upper surfaces.

The base stands on a plinth cut in ⅛in thick wood. Cut the pieces from the pattern, mitring the corners to fit. Cut strips of wood ⅛ x ³/₁₆in and glue to the underside of the base to form a framework against which to glue the plinth. Glue the plinth to the frame and the underside of the base.

Cut the drawer fronts to fit the drawer spaces, allowing a fraction of clearance all around. Use the shaper table to cut a fine decorative recess around the outside edge of the drawer fronts. Cut and assemble the drawers as described on p23. Small wooden handles whittled from ³/₁₆in blocks of wood glued to the drawer fronts were used in the example. Finally, use a craft knife to chamfer the outer edges of the sides and the upright divider as shown on the pattern.

To make the dresser top, cut two rectangular pieces for the sides and use the shaper table to cut ³/₃₂in wide grooves for the two shelves and the back before using a fret-saw to shape the curved front edges. Cut two shelves, noting that the shelves butt against the back.

Cut the back the same length as the sides. This may be made in one piece, with planking scored, or more realistically by butting ½in wide planks together.

To assemble the top (Fig 130), glue the shelves into the sides, ensuring that the front edges are flush. Glue the back into the sides and against the shelves. Check that the construction is square and allow to dry.

Cut strips of very fine wood for the plate rails (H) and glue these to the shelves ³/₁₆in from the back edge. Cut a rectangular piece (I) for the top from ¹/₁₆in thick wood and glue to the top of the sides and back. Note that this top overhangs the side and front edges by ¹/₁₆in.

Cut the decorative frieze from ³/₃₂in wood with a fret-saw and smooth the curved edges with a needle file and abrasive paper. Glue the frieze to the underside of the top so that it is recessed slightly into the sides.

To make the pediment, use ⅛ x ³/₈in wood with one edge rounded off, as shown in Fig 130. Cut two sides and a front, with mitred corners, and glue in place so that they overhang the top. Cut a similar frame in ³/₈ x ¹/₁₆in wood (without the rounded edge) and glue this to the top of the first frame to overhang.

Cut chamfers on the outside front edges of the sides with a craft knife as shown on the pattern.

To hold the dresser top securely on the base, drill two ¹/₁₆in diameter holes to a depth of ⅛in in the underside of both sides of the top. Fit pegs to protrude ⅛in. Drill corresponding holes into the top of the base to receive the pegs. Glue the top to the base. The join may be trimmed with a fine strip of decorative moulding (J). Stain and polish the assembled dresser as required.

Plate 29 KITCHEN FURNITURE

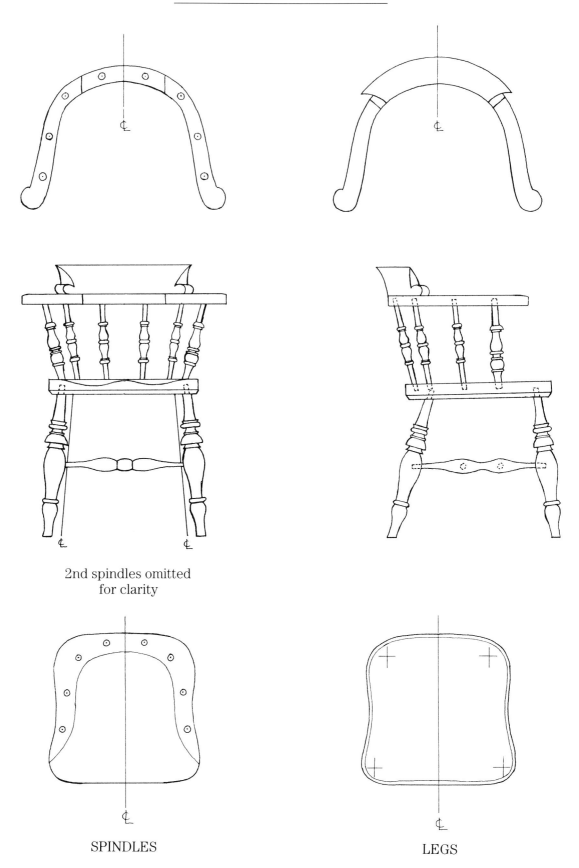

2nd spindles omitted
for clarity

SPINDLES

LEGS

Fig 131 PATTERN FOR THE SMOKER'S BOW

CHAIRS · Both chairs described here are traditional Windsor chairs. Although the shaping is different, the leg and seat assembly are the same for both chairs. Full instructions for leg and seat assembly are given for the smoker's bow, and these instructions should be used for the leg and seat assembly of the baluster-back chair.

SMOKER'S BOW · The chair seat is made from fine-grained cherry, and all the other parts are made of yew (Fig 131).

To make the seat, trace the pattern onto the wood with the grain running from back to front, marking the centre line and the position of the arm spindles in pencil. Use a fret-saw to cut the seat and clean the edge with a needle file and abrasive paper.

Mark the centre line on the underside of the seat. The centre line will be used as a guide to measure the position of the legs etc, and must be retained throughout the construction of the chair.

Mark the position of the saddling on the seat and use a craft knife with a curved blade to carve the saddling. Fig 134 shows the shape of the saddling and reference to a life-size Windsor chair will be useful. Use abrasive paper to smooth the chair seat, taking care not to remove the pencil guidelines. Cut a shallow chamfer around the edge of the underside of the seat as shown in Fig 131.

The arms are made in three pieces to ensure sufficient strength. Prepare three blocks of wood, as shown on the pattern (Fig 132a), noting that the grain runs vertically on the two arm pieces and horizontally on the back piece. Use a smear of glue to hold the three blocks temporarily together while you trace the outline of the arm assembly. Mark the centre line on the back piece and retain this line throughout assembly. Separate the three blocks and drill fine holes inside the marked outline, into each piece so that they can be pegged together. Peg and glue the three blocks together, ensuring that the marked outline is not distorted, and allow to dry thoroughly. With a fret-saw, cut out the arm assembly.

To make the crest rail, cut a curved block of wood as shown in Fig 132b, noting that the front curved edge should correspond with the front curved edge of the arm assembly. Mark the centre line and use a fret-saw to cut the shaped ears at both ends of the piece (Figs 132c and d). Clean the shaping with a craft knife and needle file.

Glue the crest rail to the arm assembly so that the front edges are flush and the marked centre lines match. The crest rail overhangs the arm assembly at the back. Use a ½in drum sander in the electric drill to shape the crest rail as shown in Fig 132e, so that the overhang is pared away in a smooth concave curve until the crest rail is flush with the arms. The front of the crest rail is pared away in a smooth convex curve to the top edge. Shape the arms so that the upper surfaces are slightly rounded and sand the assembly thoroughly.

Prepare eight 2in round blanks for the arm spindles and turn as shown on the pattern. Note that measurements for the spindle lengths should be taken from the pattern with dividers as follows: the front and second

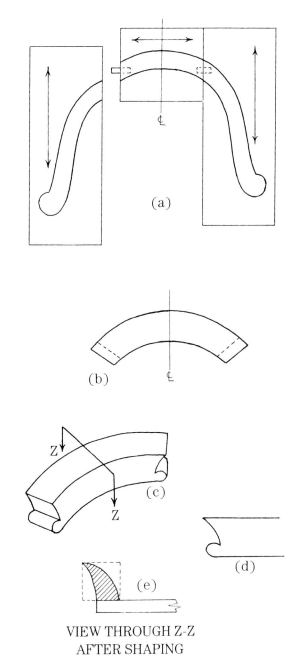

VIEW THROUGH Z-Z
AFTER SHAPING

Fig 132 CONSTRUCTION DETAILS FOR ARMS AND CREST OF SMOKER'S BOW

spindles measured from Fig 131 front elevation and the four back spindles from Fig 131 side elevation. Ensure that the spindles are turned long enough to be pegged into the arms and seat.

Make careful reference to the pattern to determine the correct angles at which the spindles fit into the seat and into the underside of the arms. Drill holes to receive the spindles. Dry-fit the front two and back two spindles into the seat. Position the arms onto these spindles and check that the angles are correct and that the assembly is symmetrical. (Note that the arms and seat are not parallel.) Remove the arms and glue the four spindles into the seat, dry-fitting the arms again to recheck the symmetry.

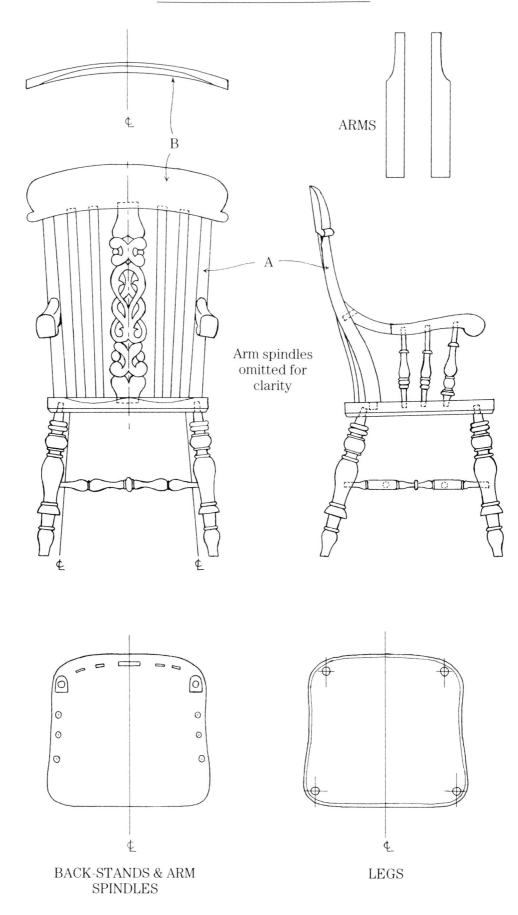

ARMS

B

A

Arm spindles
omitted for
clarity

BACK-STANDS & ARM
SPINDLES

LEGS

Fig 133 PATTERN FOR BALUSTER-BACK CHAIR

Allow to dry, then position and glue the remaining spindles into the seat, dry-fitting the arms as before to check the angles. Glue the arms onto the spindles.

Prepare four 2½in round blanks for the legs and four 2½in round blanks for the stretchers. (The chair has two cross-stretchers.) Turn the legs and stretchers as shown on the pattern, ensuring that the top of the legs and both ends of the stretchers are extended sufficiently to peg into place. The legs are fitted into the seat by whittled pegs on the top end of each leg. The shoulders of each peg are angled to fit flush against the underside of the seat (see Fig 135c).

Using the guideline on the underside of the seat, mark the position of the legs. Refer to the pattern to determine the angles and drill holes to receive the leg pegs. Glue the front legs into the seat and allow to dry thoroughly. Mark and drill holes for the side stretchers in the front and back legs (see Fig 135c) and holes in the side stretchers to receive the cross stretchers. Glue the side stretchers into the front and back legs and the back legs into the seat as one operation. Apply a little glue to the holes in the side stretchers and ease cross stretchers into place. Trim the bottom of each leg with a craft knife so that the legs rest flat on the work surface. Note when trimming the legs, that the seat is angled slightly downwards to the back and that the arms are horizontal. Stain and polish the chair as required.

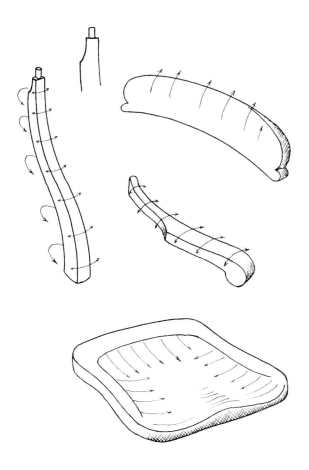

Fig 134 DETAILS OF SHAPING FOR WINDSOR CHAIRS

BALUSTER-BACK CHAIR · The chair seat is made from fine-grained cherry and all the other parts from yew (Fig 133).

Cut the seat from the pattern and use the instructions given above for the smoker's bow to mark out and shape the saddling. Mark the centre line and the position for the stands, spindles, baluster and laths.

Cut two back stands (A) from the pattern, shaping as shown in Fig 134. Note that the back edges are rounded and the front edges are slightly curved. The stands must be cut long enough to whittle a peg on the top ends to fit into the comb (B). Taper the top back edge of the stands slightly to reduce the thickness where the stand meets the comb and angle the shoulders on the pegs to follow the curve of the comb. Drill holes with a ¹⁄₁₆in bit into the lower ends of the stands to a depth of ⅛in to receive pegs which will fit the stands into the seat. Before fitting the pegs, make careful reference to Fig 133 to determine the correct angle at which the stands fit onto the seat. Trim the bottom of the stands to this angle, then cut and glue the pegs in place with ³⁄₃₂in protruding.

Cut the comb (B) from a block of yew, using the pattern as a guide for the size and shape of the curve. With a craft knife and needle file, shape the comb so that the outer edges and bottom edge retain the full thickness shown on the pattern and the piece tapers to a narrow rounded top edge. Drill holes in the underside of the comb to receive the pegs on the back stands. Mark and cut slots in the underside of the comb with a watchmaker's 'chisel' to receive the laths and baluster – the laths are ½in thick, the baluster is slightly thicker and will be tapered to fit the slot.

To make the baluster, prepare a block of yew, ½in wide and ⅜in thick and slightly longer than the baluster. Trace the profile outline (Fig 135a) onto the side of the wood block and use a fret-saw to cut the curved blank. Smooth both surfaces of the blank and check that the piece is not warped and is of uniform thickness. Trace the pattern onto the blank, leaving sufficient room at the top and bottom to slot the baluster into the seat and comb (approximately ¹⁄₁₆in at each end). The small cut-outs in the centre of the design are cut before the outside edges. Drill holes with a very fine drill bit into the centre of each cut-out to insert the fret-saw blade. Use the finest blade you can find and cut as close to the pattern line as possible, but do not distort sharp corners. Refine the shape with the tip of a pointed craft knife blade. When the cut-outs are made, cut the outer edges with a fret-saw and refine with a craft knife and needle file. Note that because of the curved profile of this piece, it is very delicate and must be worked gently. With a craft knife, carve the detail as shown in Fig 135b to give the pattern a three-dimensional effect. Taper the top back edge of the baluster slightly to fit into the slot in the comb.

Using the same profile as the baluster, cut four laths ½in thick, ensuring that sufficient length is allowed at the top and bottom to slot into the seat and comb.

Drill holes into the seat to receive the back stands and cut slots in the seat to receive the baluster and laths.

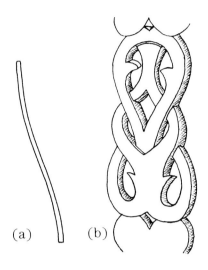

(a) (b)

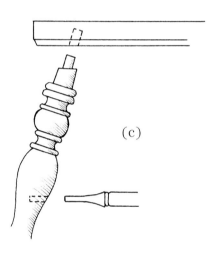

(c)

Fig 135 (A) PROFILE FOR BALUSTER AND LATHS; (B) DETAIL
OF BALUSTER; (C) PEGGING LEGS AND STRETCHERS

Dry-fit the back stands, baluster and comb and check
that the angles are correct and the assembly is symmetrical. Remove the comb and glue the stands into the seat,
replacing the comb to recheck the symmetry. Glue the
baluster into the seat, again with the comb in place to
check the symmetry. Allow to dry thoroughly, then glue
the laths into the seat and the comb onto the laths,
baluster and stands.

Prepare six 1½in round blanks for the arm spindles.
Turn these as shown on the pattern, leaving sufficient
length at each end to peg the spindles into the seat and
the arms.

Cut a pair of arms as shown on the pattern, noting the
profile as shown on the side elevation. Round off the top
edge of the arms as shown in Fig 134 and shape the back
edges to follow the profile of the back stands. Drill holes
into the underside of the arms and into the seat to receive
the spindles. With the spindles dry-fitted into the arms,
glue the spindles into the seat, noting that they angle
slightly outwards. The arms should rest tightly against
the back stands. Glue the arms onto the spindles and to
the back stands and allow to dry thoroughly. Drill small
holes through the arms and into the back stands as
shown on the pattern and glue pegs into these holes to
secure the arms to the stands. When dry, trim the pegs
flush with the arms.

Cut and turn the legs and stretchers from the pattern
and assemble and glue into the seat as described above
for the smoker's bow. Stain and polish the chair as required.

ACCESSORIES

CLOTHES-AIRER · The clothes-airer (Fig 136) is made of
pine or any similar light-coloured wood. Cut two ends
from ⅛in thick wood with a fret-saw. Mark the position of
the holes and drill the holes through both pieces at once
to ensure symmetry, with a ³⁄₃₂in drill bit. Prepare four

Fig 136 PATTERN AND ASSEMBLY FOR THE CLOTHES-AIRER

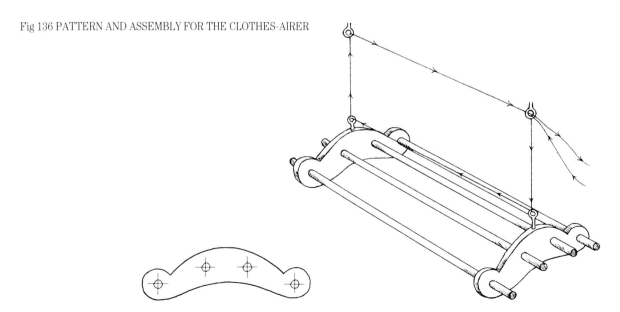

172

4½in rails, ⅜in in diameter (these are best prepared from ⅜in square wood using a craft knife to round the corners and abrasive paper to smooth the shape). Glue the rails into the ends so that ¼in protrudes at each end and check that the assembly lies flat on the work surface. Screw ⅛in diameter eye-hooks into the top of both ends. The clothes-airer was sanded but not stained or polished. Hang the airer from eye-hooks screwed into the ceiling above the hooks in the airer, using linen thread for the cords. The ends of the cords are wound around a hook glued to the side of the chimney-breast.

The washboard, the rolling-pin and pastry-board and the bread-board are made from obeche wood and dowelling. The bread is moulded in bread paste and baked in the oven. The broom is made in the same way as the one described on p116. The miniature shirt on the clothes-airer is made in cotton lawn with bead buttons (see Chapter 7, p93). The tea-towels are fringed lengths of cotton tape and the tablecloth is a fringed square of cotton gingham.

The grandfather clock is made from a kit from Jennifer's of Walsall and the gun is a painted white metal miniature from Phoenix Model Developments. The fine porcelain willow-pattern service on the dresser is from The Dolls' House, and all the copper and brass pans are from Country Treasures.

The warming-pan and the beer barrel on a stand are from Sussex Crafts and the vegetables and the pair of pheasants hanging from the beam are from Rohanna Bryan. The roller towel, the bucket under the sink and the marmalade cat sitting on the chair are from Dorking Dolls' House Gallery and the Toby jug on the mantleshelf is from Polly Flinders.

Joan Dodd embroidered the needlepoint picture above the hearth and Leo Pilley made the glass demijohn on the draining-board. The stoneware hot-water bottle and storage jars are from Carol Lodder, the carpet beater from C & D Crafts and the pot of jam on the table from Thames Valley Crafts. The bowl of eggs, the trivet, the kitchen knives and cleaver and the sack of flour are from Quality Dolls' House Miniatures.

The accessories described are all fine-quality miniatures chosen from the ranges supplied by the stockists named (see pp175–9).

MAGAZINES, STOCKISTS, FAIRS & BOOKS

The dolls' house hobby has grown so popular in the UK and US, and more recently in Australia, that there are now shops everywhere and it would be impossible to list them all. If you are new to the hobby, we advise that you subscribe to one of the dolls' house magazines or directories listed here, where you will find information about shops in your area.

Please include an SAE or IRC with all enquiries.

UK SUPPLIERS AND MAGAZINES

For a comprehensive list of UK craftspeople and suppliers, we recommend that you contact:

The Dolls' House Information Service, Avalon Court, Star Road, Partridge Green, West Sussex RH13 8RY
Telephone: (0403) 711511
or
The Dollshouse Hobby Directory, 25 Priory Road, Kew Green, Richmond, Surrey TW9 3DW

The list of stockists on the following pages has been revised and updated (1994). A few of the suppliers mentioned in the book are no longer in business. Others, such as Thames Valley Crafts, now supply through dolls' house shops all over the country. The small ads in the dolls' house magazines are a constantly up-to-date reference source.

MAGAZINES

The following magazines are specialist dolls' house publications which contain a wealth of information including articles, how-to projects, advertising and listings of dolls' house fairs around the country. They are available on subscription from the addresses below:

Dolls' House World, Avalon Court, Star Road, Partridge Green, West Sussex RH13 8RY (Telephone: 0403 711511)

The International Dolls House News, PO Box 154, Cobham, Surrey KT11 2YE (Telephone: 0932 867938)

The Home Miniaturist, Avalon Court, Star Road, Partridge Green, West Sussex RH13 8RY (Telephone: 0403 711511)

Dolls' House and Miniature Scene, 5 Cissbury Road, Ferring, West Sussex BN12 6OJ (Telephone: 0903 506626) (also available from W.H. Smith)

For a very wide-ranging catalogue of books on dolls' houses, miniatures, architecture, crafts and furnishings, contact:

The Mulberry Bush, 9 George Street, Brighton, Sussex BN2 1RH
(Telephone: 0273 493781/600471)

One other publication which is very useful is the Hobby's catalogue. This is published annually in the autumn and is available from newsagents (including W. H. Smith) and model shops, or from W. Hobby Ltd, Knight's Hill Square, London SE27 0HH (Telephone: (081) 761 4244). Hobby's sell a wide range of tools and materials for the miniaturist which are all available by mail order from the catalogue.

SHOPS

The following shops are open to the public during business hours and all produce a catalogue/price list and provide a mail order service. (Where the shop attends a fair(s), the fair is given in brackets at the end of the listing.)
NB: 'W' at the end of an entry denotes that the supplier also sells wholesale. 'E' indicates a supplier who exports his products.

Blackwells of Hawkwell, 733 London Road, Westcliffe on Sea, Essex SS0 9ST
Telephone: (0702) 72248. Open 9am–5.30pm, Monday, Tuesday, Thursday, Friday, Saturday
Furniture kits, wallpapers, carpets, wood-mouldings, hand tools, power tools, lighting, hardwoods, glues, stains, etc; also model-railway equipment.   W   E

The Dolls' House, 29 The Market, Covent Garden, London WC2 8RE

Telephone: (071) 379 7243. Open 10am–8pm, Monday to Saturday

Craftsman-made British dolls' houses and miniatures including many exclusive items. Also budget-priced imported miniatures. Commissions accepted for dolls' houses and miniatures. England's first specialist shop. (Kensington)   E

Dolphin Miniatures, Myrtle Cottage, Greendown, Membury, Axminster, Devon EX13 7TB

Telephone: (040-488) 459. Open 9am to dusk every day except Christmas

Small shop selling own craftsman-made miniatures including dolls' houses, furniture, rocking-horses, ship models and tiny tools. Commissions accepted. (London, Lyndhurst, Exeter, Cornwall)   W   E

Dorking Dolls' House Gallery, 23 West Street, Dorking, Surrey RH4 1BY

Telephone: (0306) 885 785. Open 10am–5pm, Tuesday, Thursday, Friday, Saturday

DIY materials and wallpapers, furniture, accessories, dolls, including many exclusive items. Miniatures for children and collectors. Books. Commissions accepted. (Dorking, Farnham, Windsor, Cobham)   E

Jennifer's of Walsall, Graingers, 51 George Street, Walsall, West Midlands

Telephone: (0922) 23382. Open 9am–5.30pm, Monday to Saturday

Building materials, dolls' house plans, hardwoods, furniture kits, tools, lighting, wallpaper, furniture and accessories, including exclusive items. (Kensington, Harrogate, Birmingham)   E

Leo Pilley, Chy An Chy Glass Studio, St Ives, Cornwall

Telephone: (0736) 797659. Open 10am–5.30pm, Monday, Tuesday, Wednesday, Friday, Saturday

Miniature hand-blown glass items including bottles, vases with flowers, dishes, jugs, candlesticks, etc. Commissions accepted during the winter months. (London, Dorking, Birmingham)

Mini Mansions, 10 The Hawthorns, Great Ayton, Middlesbrough, Cleveland TS9 6BA

Telephone: (0642) 723060. Open 10am–5pm, Tuesday to Saturday

Home showroom open to the public. Fine craftsman-made miniatures, silver, china, glass and pottery, DIY supplies, white metal kits, wallpaper. Commissions accepted. (London, Dorking, Birmingham, Harrogate, Norfolk, York)   W   E

The Mulberry Bush, 25 Trafalgar Street, Brighton, Sussex BN1 4EQ

Telephone: (0273) 600471. Open 10am–5pm, Tuesday, Thursday, Friday, Saturday

Dolls' houses, furniture, accessories. DIY materials including brass fittings, mouldings, tools, lighting, dolls. Large stock of specialist books. Commissions accepted. (Most fairs in the South and Midlands)   W   E

Recollect Studios, The Old School, London Road, Sayers Common, West Sussex BN6 9HX

Telephone: (0273) 833314. Open 10am–5pm, Tuesday to Saturday

Miniature accessories, also porcelain doll-making materials and kits. Doll-making and china painting courses.   W   E

The Singing Tree, 69 New King's Road, London SW6 45Q

Telephone: (071) 736 4527. Open 10am-5.30pm, Monday to Saturday

Old and new doll's houses, DIY materials, wallpapers, etc. Wide range of miniatures. Hiring service. (Kensington)   W   E

MAIL ORDER SUPPLIERS

The following stockists supply a range of miniatures and sell by mail order. They all produce a catalogue, but they do *not* have shops open to the public. (Where the supplier attends a fair(s), the fair is given in brackets at the end of the listing.)

Mini Marvels, 25 Crescent View, Leeds LS17 7QF

Telephone: (0532) 679521

Miniature woven Turkish rugs and carpets. (London, Birmingham)   W   E

Phoenix Model Developments, The Square, Earls Barton, Northampton NN6 0NA

Telephone: (0604) 810612

A wide range of own cast, white metal kits including fireplaces, fittings, utensils, mangle, kitchen range, sewing-machine, etc.   W   E

The Dolls' House Draper, PO Box 128, Lightcliffe, Halifax, W. Yorkshire HX3 8RN

Telephone: (0422) 201275

Have taken over from Sunday Dolls – supplying an enormous range of fine ribbons, laces, tools, fabrics and trimmings for dressmaking and soft furnishing. Also patterns and materials for miniature knitting. (Birmingham, Kensington)   W

Sussex Crafts, 6 Robinson Road, Crawley, West Sussex RH11 7AD
Telephone: (0293) 548725
A range of miniatures made by own craftsmen including kitchen, scullery and bathroom items, fireplaces, flooring, brickwork, plumbing, hardware and building components; also geyser and kitchen range. Commissions accepted. (Kensington)   E

Wood 'n Wool Miniatures, Yew Tree House, 3 Stankelt Road, Silverdale, Carnforth, Lancashire LA5 0RB
Telephone: (0524) 701532. (Home showroom open by appointment)
Specialists in dolls' house lighting. Ready-made furniture and kits, DIY materials including mouldings, brass hardware and accessories. Lights, lighting kits and instruction book on copper-tape wiring system. (London, Birmingham, Harrogate, Dorking, Marlborough)   W   E

SPECIALISTS

The following suppliers specialise in one aspect of miniatures, usually craftsmen making and selling their own work. They all produce a catalogue/price list and provide a mail order service but (unless otherwise noted) they are not open to the public. (Where the specialist attends a fair(s), the fair is given in brackets at the end of the listing.)

Isabel Wood, 'Rosemead', Tarporley Road, Clotton, Tarporley, Cheshire CW6 0CG (write for details).
Fine, undressed character dolls made to commission.

Sunday Dolls, 7 Park Drive, East Sheen, London SW14 8RB
Telephone: (081) 876-5634
Exquisitely dressed dolls' house dolls of every period, made to commission. (Kensington)   E
Haberdashery now sold by The Dolls' House Draper.

C & D Crafts, 133 Lower Hillmorton Road, Rugby, Warwickshire CV21 3TN
Telephone: (0788) 74540. Visitors by appointment
Miniature cane-work baskets and accessories including babies' cots with bedding and mini bicycles with baskets. Commissions accepted. (London, Lyndhurst, Norwich)   W   E

Carol Lodder, Brooks Cottage, Belchalwell, Blandford, Dorset DT11 0EG
Telephone: (0258) 860 222. Pottery open by appointment
Hand-thrown pottery miniatures, hand-decorated fine porcelain, Delftware, stoneware, old English slipware. Also country furniture pieces and room-settings. Commissions accepted. (London, Dorking, Lyndhurst)   W   E

Reuben Barrows, 30 Wolsey Gardens, Hainault, Ilford, Essex IG6 2SN
Telephone: (0992) 719593
Interior and exterior moulded claddings including brick, slate, roof tiles and 'oak panelling'. (Kensington)   W

Country Treasures, Rose Cottage, Dapple Heath, Admaston, near Rugely, Staffs WS15 3PG
Telephone: (088-921) 652. (Visitors by appointment)
A wide range of brass and copper kitchenware including kettles, saucepans and scales; also plates and assorted foodstuffs. (London, Leeds, Birmingham, Dorking, Harrogate)   W   E

Isobel Hockey, 12 Lancaster Road, Maybush, Southampton SO1 6DP
Telephone: (0703) 784314
Hand-knitted dolls' clothes, in fine wool and cotton including baby-doll layettes. Commissions accepted. (Lyndhurst)

Terence Stringer, Spindles, Lexham Road, Litcham, Norfolk PE32 2QQ
Telephone: (0328) 701891
A wide range of items in turned wood with bone, silver and mother of pearl including sewing items, desk accessories and toys. (Kensington, Birmingham, Lyndhurst, Marlborough).   W   E

Vale Dolls Houses, 'Wayside', Church Street, Whatton in the Vale, Nottingham NG13 9EL
Telephone: (0949) 50365
A wide range of good quality whitewood dolls' houses and houses made to commission. (Birmingham, Kensington)

WHOLESALE SUPPLIERS

The suppliers listed below are wholesalers but their miniatures are available from many of the retailers listed above.

Dijon (Importers) Ltd, The Old Print Works, Heathfield, Sussex TN21 8HX
Telephone: (0435) 864155. (Visitors by appointment)
Large range of furniture, accessories, DIY materials, wallpaper, lighting, kits, dolls. (Birmingham, London)   E

Quality Dolls' House Miniatures, 55 Celandine Avenue, Priory Park, Locksheath, nr Southampton SO3 6WZ
Telephone: (04895) 78420
Handmade food items, painted cast white metal kitchen utensils, garden tools, cats, clocks, etc. (Retail sales at fairs: London, Birmingham, Windsor, Farnham, Cobham, Lyndhurst, Dorking)   E

MAGAZINES, STOCKISTS, FAIRS & BOOKS

AUSTRALIAN SUPPLIERS AND MAGAZINES

In Australia, the dolls' house hobby is fairly new, but growing rapidly and there are many specialist shops, mail order suppliers and craftspeople, but as the country is so large, we suggest that you contact *The Australian Miniaturist Magazine* as a starting point. The address is: 40 Cusack Street, Wangaratta, Victoria 3677.

UK magazines (see above) can also be sent to subscribers in Australia, and contain much information which is relevant to them. Most UK suppliers will send catalogues and goods to Australia – but please enclose an IRC with all enquiries.

US SUPPLIERS AND MAGAZINES

In the US, the dolls' house hobby is so widespread that there are literally thousands of suppliers. The beginner is advised to look for a local miniatures shop which will probably stock most things needed for the projects in this book. For more information, there is an annual mail order suppliers directory called *The Miniatures Catalogue* which can be ordered from: Hobby Book Distributors, 3150 State Line Road, North Bend, Ohio 45052. This address is also the US office of *Dolls' House World* magazine.

Small ads can be found in all the miniatures publications for suppliers of the tools and materials required for the projects in the book.

MINIATURES FAIRS – BUYING AND SELLING

Well-established miniatures fairs now take place all over the country. Miniatura in Birmingham and The London Dolls' House Festival in Kensington are the major fairs, but there are smaller events everywhere, advertised locally or through the specialist magazines.

For anyone interested in miniatures, a fair is a wonderful day out. The admission price is generally very modest and one can have a splendid time just browsing. The fair offers the opportunity to see the work of craftsmen, compare prices, pick up new ideas and talk to other people who share your interest. You will see a wide range of miniatures, from things which make you feel smug about your own work to things so fine that you wonder how human hands can make them.

Fairs also provide the perfect opportunity for miniaturists to sell their own work. If you produce miniatures of sufficient quality and in sufficient quantity that you would like to sell, contact the fair organiser to book a stall. Selling at a fair is a good way to begin as you sell direct to the customer, so once your stall fee is paid, the profits are yours. Although stall fees at the major fairs can be expensive and generally one has to be invited to exhibit, smaller local events are a different matter. Once you have booked a stall, you will need sufficient stock to fill it and you will need to price it. Check at other fairs to get some idea of the price of similar goods. You must cover your costs and make some profit, otherwise selling

is pointless, but it is a sad fact of life that the skills required to make good miniatures are often undervalued. If you do well, you may find that making miniatures for sale can become a lucrative part-time or even full-time job, and you may prefer to sell through one or more of the specialist shops. This involves a greater degree of commitment, but offers some security as, provided your work sells, you will have repeat orders. If you sell through shops, your work must be costed on a wholesale basis. Approach the shop with samples and wholesale prices and a very clear idea of the amount of work you are prepared to commit yourself to producing. Most professional miniaturists began in a small way, selling at fairs or through a shop; others choose to sell directly to the public through their own catalogues and by advertising in the specialist magazines.

Don't be disheartened if you don't do well at the first fair or the first shop you try – they all have different characters and what will simply not sell in one place might go like 'hot cakes' somewhere else – time and experience will tell. If your work simply does not sell, consider three points:

a) Are you making the sort of things people want to buy?
b) Is the price right?
c) Are you making it well enough?

Eavesdrop on your customers – it can be very enlightening.

FAIRS

The two major fairs in Britain are Miniatura and the London Dolls' House Festival. Practically everything the miniatures world has to offer can be seen at either of these fairs.

Miniatura is a two-day event, covering the whole spectrum of miniatures in every price range, held in Birmingham every year in the spring and autumn; and Scottish Miniatura is held in June. For full details contact:

Bob & Muriel Hopwood, 41 Eastbourne Avenue, Hodge Hill, Birmingham B34 6AR (Tel: 021 783 2070)

The London Dolls' House Festival is a three-day event held in Kensington in May each year; it offers an enormous range of fine quality miniatures. The festival also publishes a directory of shops and craftsmen, covering the whole country. For details of the festival or the directory contact:

Caroline Hamilton, 25 Priory Road, Kew Green, Richmond TW9 3DQ (Tel: 081 948 1893)

Both these fairs exhibit the best of British miniatures and also include a number of guest exhibitors from abroad.

They both have 'limited entry' days with tickets bought in advance, and 'open' days when tickets can be bought at the door.

(Please enclose an SAE with all enquiries.)

Among the other well-established fairs are those at Marlborough (November), Lyndhurst (April, October), Dorking (June) and Farnham (April, November).

There are also smaller events all over the country, some of which specialise in miniatures, others which combine miniatures with dolls or toys.

Smaller fairs are usually one-day events and generally have a range of exhibitors, including craftsmen, suppliers and often local dolls' house clubs.

There are now so many fairs that it is not practical to list them, but they all advertise in the specialist magazines – giving details of the dates, venue and organiser. Some fairs have prepaid 'limited entry' tickets for the first hour or two, and these are an excellent idea if you dislike crowds.

BOOKS

If you are building, decorating and furnishing a dolls' house, you may find the following books useful:

Making Dolls' House Interiors by Carol and Nigel Lodder, published by David & Charles (1994)

The New Dolls' House DIY Book by Venus & Martin Dodge, published by David & Charles (1993)

Making and Dressing Dolls' House Dolls by Sue Atkinson, published by David & Charles (1992)

Home Comfort by Christina Hardyment, published by Viking/National Trust (1992)

Making Dolls' Houses by Brian Nickolls, published by David & Charles (1991)

The Elements of Style by Stephen Calloway, published by Mitchell Beazley (1991)

The Dolls' Dressmaker by Venus Dodge, published by David & Charles (1987)

The English Home by Doreen Yarwood, published by Batsford (1979)

INDEX

Numbers in *italics* refer to illustrations

INDEX